THE WILLPOWER ADVANTAGE

TOM PETERSON and RYAN HANNING

The WillPower Advantage

Building Habits for Lasting Happiness

IGNATIUS PRESS   SAN FRANCISCO

Cover art by Holly Jonas

Cover design by Enrique J. Aguilar

© 2020 by Amen Alleluia, Inc., Roswell, Georgia
Published 2020 by Ignatius Press, San Francisco
All rights reserved
ISBN 978-1-62164-422-4 (PB)
ISBN 978-1-64229-140-7 (eBook)
Library of Congress Control Number 2020933464
Printed in the United States of America ∞

CONTENTS

Part 3

Your Action Plan with God

Part I

We Are Made for So Much More

I

Why Me? Why Now?

"I came that they might have life, and have it more abundantly."

—John 10:10

We all want more peace and joy in life, but the chaos of our busy world seems to impede our progress. All around us, self-discipline and the daily work ethic have been replaced by self-centeredness and around-the-clock personal entertainment. As a result, the willingness and the ability to make sacrifices for faith and family have become scarce, and so too have joy and peace. This book is a means of help and a call to action for fighting the behaviors that silently drain our happiness and steal our joy by enslaving us to things that can never fulfill us.

The WillPower Advantage is neither pop psychology nor watered-down Christianity; rather, it is a lifestyle reboot that can enable us to respond better to Christ's call to follow Him. As disciples of Jesus, we can claim ourselves, our families, our cities, and our culture for Christ. To help us with this task, we have an invaluable resource in the age-old wisdom of the Church.

Three Important Questions

Imagine for a moment what life would be like if more Christians lived more authentically just a small portion of Jesus' teaching and example. How would the world be different? What would change if we followed more closely Christ's call to forgive others, feed the

9

poor, and love our enemies? What would improve if we put into practice the virtuous actions that we all know we should do, but often fail to do? The truth is, when we do God's will, we bring a little taste of heaven down to earth.

Consider the generosity and the kindness of the Good Samaritan (Lk 10:25–37); the compassion of the father toward the Prodigal Son (Lk 15:11–32); Jesus' own example of humility in washing the apostles' feet (Jn 13:1–17); His forgiveness of those who persecuted and killed Him (Lk 23:34); and, ultimately, His self-sacrificial love on the cross (Jn 15:13). This list could go on and on. The Gospels, and the entire narrative of salvation history throughout the Old and New Testaments, have compelled faithful followers to love and to serve God and others. This is the raison d'être and the basic mission of the Church, as Pope Benedict XVI said: "The Church is missionary by nature and her principal task is evangelization, which aims to proclaim and to witness to Christ and to promote his Gospel of peace and love in every environment and culture."[1]

Praise God that many earnest Christians throughout history have indeed followed the Lord. But we all know that exemplary Christians have often been the exception and not the rule. As G. K. Chesterton said, "The Christian ideal has not been tried and found wanting. It has been found difficult; and left untried."[2]

Ask yourself these reflective questions:

Q. How would the world be different if we followed Christ more completely?
Q. What would change in my life if I followed Christ's words more faithfully?
  • Would I have more or less peace and joy in my life?
  • Would I be more or less of a father, mother, brother, sister, daughter, son?
  • Would I be more or less free?
  • Would I be more or less happy?

The Christian faith has always been about accepting God's loving gift of salvation, along with the forgiveness and the freedom that He won for us through the atoning sacrifice of Christ. However, accepting this gift means cooperating with God's grace in order to become like Christ. Imagine a child receiving a wonderful gift wrapped in elegant paper and topped with an elaborate bow. The giver of the gift took care to wrap the package beautifully, indicating that what is inside is equally thoughtful and even more valuable. Now imagine the child never opening the present, never using it. Did the child receive the gift? Likewise, if we only admire the gift of our salvation from the outside and never open it, never put its power to use in our lives, have we accepted it? No, we haven't. Furthermore, we have missed the point of receiving God's gifts. The gifts of salvation and of faith are not just to be admired passively, but to be cultivated so that they can grow in our lives.

Let's go back to that second question: "What would change in my life if I followed Christ's words more faithfully?" The answer is "Everything!" Every aspect of my life would be filled with both the struggle and the grace to grow into the person God made me to be. This really is good news. No, this is fantastic news! God has a plan for each one of us, and He wants us to become the person He created us to be. This is the same fantastic news that spread like a wildfire throughout the Roman Empire two thousand years ago and has been burning in the hearts of faithful Christians to this day.

These first two questions: "How would the world be different if we followed Christ's teaching more completely?" and "What would change in my life if I followed Christ's words more faithfully?" are naturally followed by a third question: "Why don't we do something about it?" Our inaction is not primarily due to a lack of knowledge, as we are aware of the problems and the actions we should be taking to address them. Nor is it due to a lack of desire, or will, for we all want to live better lives. Then what's the issue? College Football Hall of Fame Coach Bear Bryant of Alabama said, "It's not the will to win that matters. Everyone has that. *It's the will to prepare to win that matters.*"[3] It is true in our careers, it is true in our personal lives, and it is true in matters of faith. Master your thoughts ∆ life experience

God's grace and our cooperative diligence can work in unison to bring more blessings into our lives and the world around us. But first we must align our will with God's perfect will for us, so that we can respond in love and truth to our own personal challenges, and those of the human family. *The WillPower Advantage* has been designed to help you *prepare* to win—to prepare to win the spiritual war, to prepare to win the battle against bad habits. And it does this by helping you to conform your will to God's will for your life.

Let us be honest, there are many good people in this world, and there are many devout Christians, but *not* every single person is striving to become the person God created him to be. Why? Because we all struggle with sin. Each one of us has fallen for the custom-made lies that trick us into believing that we are something less than we are. The Father of Lies, the devil, baits his hooks with custom-made fishing lures to snag us and lead us away from God. The truth is, we all have been created by God in His image (Gen 1:27). And each of us is a unique and unrepeatable individual destined by God to be conformed to the image of His Son (Rom 8:29). We were made for something more than enslavement to bad habits. We all know this deep down. It is worth saying again: *we were made for something more*. As Saint John Paul II said, "*We are not the sum of our weaknesses and failures*; we are the sum of the Father's love for us and our real capacity to become the image of His Son."[4]

One way we know we were made for something more is that we desire more. The ancient philosopher Plato would say that we all desire perfect truth, perfect beauty, perfect goodness, perfect love, and perfect wholeness. Yet these desires cannot be completely fulfilled in this imperfect world. The truth, beauty, and goodness that we experience in this world can only point us toward the source of our fulfilment. The world is good; in fact, God said it is "very good" (Gen 1:31). God calls us to care for it and to work out our salvation in it, even though it is not enough to make us perfectly happy. C. S. Lewis, the great English author and theologian, explained it well when he said, "If I find in myself a desire which no experience in this world can satisfy, the most probable explanation is that I was made for another world."[5] We repeat, we are made for something more.

But how do we find this something more, this other world? Jesus said that He is "the way, and the truth, and the life" (Jn 14:6). The challenge is to take Him at His word and to do the daily work of following Him. By doing that, we become the person each one of us is called to be. Now that we have reminded ourselves of this, let's change our third question from "Why don't we do something about it?" to "What am I going to do about it?"

So let's review our three big questions. They should be on the hearts and minds of every Christian.

1. How would the world be different if we followed Christ's teaching more completely?
2. What would change in my life if I followed Christ's words more faithfully?
3. What am I going to do about it? (Don't sweat it; we're here to help you with this one.)

Four Forgotten Truths

Why are these three questions so important for us today? The simple answer is because we have forgotten who we are. Why? Because we have been distracted by the chaos and the noise of the world. We have been deceived by the spiritual warfare surrounding us every hour of every day, which we barely perceive. We have been desensitized by an unrelenting deluge of secularism in the media and in our culture, which creates the currents of beliefs, values, and trends we swim in. Christians need help with living out the Gospel in this modern age, which is often referred to as the "post-Christian age". This is not a harsh judgment but an honest evaluation.

The WillPower Advantage provides help to everyday Christians who want to live more like Christ. It offers a way for rediscovering the adventure, the beauty, and the joy of a Christian life well lived. It invites us to reflect on the three central questions mentioned above and reminds us of four forgotten truths:

1. God wants us to be happy.
2. The Christian life takes work.
3. Grace builds upon nature.
4. We were never meant to go through life alone. (God sent the Holy Spirit to guide us and His Church until the end of time!)

Both of us authors must confess that we wrote this book with ourselves in mind. We live in two of the busiest and largest cities in America, Atlanta and Nashville, which are filled with unnerving, unending traffic. And, when we get upset in traffic, our blood pressure goes up, our patience evaporates, and we often start yelling and swearing at the other drivers. Yet the problem is *not the traffic*; it is our response to it.

Rather than purchasing more religious medals for the visor or advising other drivers about how they can drive more to our liking, we need to change our response to the situation. How? By working with the gifts God gives us, participating with His grace, and using the traffic as an opportunity to become more like Christ. This participation is different from the quick spiritual fix that we often seek. God wants us to respond to His grace and to do the work necessary to become the person He made us to be.

"But I'm only human," you say. "If I yell at the other drivers and teach them a thing or two about driving properly, because after all they are lousy drivers, I will feel better!" But that thinking never really helps! In fact, it often leads to foolishness and sin.

Our life is not a problem to be solved, but rather a quest for virtue. Only by cultivating the good and growing into the person we were created to become can we be truly happy. Really! (By the way, do not be discouraged if this sounds daunting, because we have lots of good practical advice and information in the upcoming chapters, which will shed light on this quest and make the journey easier.)

Jesus used agricultural analogies, because they were relevant to the agrarian people of His time and place, but these analogies offer wisdom to us city dwellers, as well. Here is an example. Jesus said, "I am the true vine, and my Father is the vinedresser. Every branch of mine that bears no fruit, he takes away, and every branch that does bear fruit he prunes, that it may bear more fruit" (Jn 15:1–2). Jesus describes discipleship not as working toward an academic degree or a career goal, but as growing and being pruned. When a gardener prunes a plant, he cuts off the branches that are unhealthy or have not produced fruit. That way the energy the plant expends can go to the branches that are producing fruit. So, too, with us. With our cooperation, the Lord prunes aspects of our lives that do not bear fruit, so that we can focus on growing those things that make us into the person God calls us to be.

Saint Paul summed up the unfruitful branches and the fruitful ones this way: "The works of the flesh are plain: immorality, impurity, licentiousness, idolatry, sorcery, enmity, strife, jealousy, anger, self-ishness, dissension, party spirit, envy, drunkenness, carousing, and the like.... But the fruit of the Spirit is love, joy, peace, patience, kindness, goodness, faithfulness, gentleness, self-control" (Gal 5:19–23). In this context, the word *flesh* means our fallen human nature that has a tendency toward evil.

So how do we let the Lord prune the bad and cultivate the good? How do I allow what God has given me—my temperament, my experiences, and my situation in life—to become the raw material that He uses to make me the person He created me to be? What does that look like? Perhaps it can be summed up with a quote commonly attributed to Saint Augustine, arguably one of history's most famous converts: "Know thyself, and thy faults, and thus live!" In other words, knowing yourself and your weaknesses, which is the heart of humility, is the starting point for training daily to choose what is good, beautiful, and true. Humility provides the rich soil in which the other virtues grow!

The way we see it, you have four options when you are confronting a challenge.

1. You can ignore it

No doubt you know people who prefer this model for dealing with challenges. Perhaps you have even tried this approach yourself.

2. You can medicate yourself

This option often goes hand in hand with option 1. There are many ways of medicating ourselves. Many cartons of ice cream or whole pumpkin pies or six-packs of beer or *worse things* have been consumed using this approach. Binge-watching sports, shows, or news also can have a drug-like effect, and so can excessive online activities such as gaming, shopping, or gazing at social media. Need we even mention pornography?

Both ignoring and medicating are passive, that is, they fail to engage us in confronting the challenge, and neither option produces growth. They do not form or strengthen your heart, mind, or body; in fact, they can deform and weaken them. But boy, they are easier than doing anything constructive and seem so attractive at first glance.

3. You can confront the problem unequipped

By unequipped we mean without the skills, knowledge, and grit needed to confront the challenge successfully. While this is an active approach, it is more likely to end in failure and discouragement, leading you right back to options 1 and 2.

4. You can confront the challenge well equipped

Well equipped means having wisdom, self-control, courage, and so on. This of course is the only option that produces personal growth.

We all have challenges we must strive to overcome, and most of these are interior challenges. They are about how we see and understand ourselves, the world, and our place in it. The challenges of our own hearts and minds are the most intimate and the most important. They are where we encounter God and grow to be more like Him. We therefore ought to pay attention to them.

Facing our interior challenges is how conversion, or turning toward God, takes place. Some challenges are innate, a result of our temperament, while others are the result of choices we have made or wounds we have received. Whatever the challenge may be, after it has been acknowledged, the formation of your will is the first step to overcoming it. Of course, God's grace, that is to say, His gifts, are needed to form the will. Grace does not destroy nature, but perfects it. God's grace builds on the foundation of the goodness of His creation. And this assurance is at the heart of *The WillPower Advantage*.

This is not a modern self-help book based on some new technique or new knowledge, but rather a participation in how God has made us and what He wills for each one of us. This is not pop-Christianity or pop-psychology, but rather ancient truths from the riches of our Christian faith. These truths can help us to overcome the bad habits that drain our happiness and steal our peace, that prick our wounds and hinder our freedom, and to direct our wills to becoming the Christlike person God has called each one of us to be. This is why Saint Paul said, "Do not be conformed to this world but be transformed by the renewal of your mind, that you may prove what is the will of God, what is good and acceptable and perfect" (Rom 12:2).

Christians, we have forgotten who we are: children of our heavenly Father, the one true God, who created us, redeemed us, sanctifies us, and loves us more than we can ever imagine or understand! Christians, we have forgotten our heritage! Now is the time to reclaim it so that we can grow into Christ by building the virtues, the good habits, that lead to true happiness. Think of the challenges you face in accepting God's invitation and opportunity to grow beyond frustration, fatigue, and woundedness, and to enter His abundant life. The famous words of Leon Bloy ring true in every generation: "The only real sadness, the only real failure, the only great tragedy in life, is not to become a saint."[6] Come join us in the adventure of growing in virtue and hope with *The WillPower Advantage.*

2

Knowing the Battle

"Put on the whole armor of God, that you may be able to
stand against the wiles of the devil."

—Ephesians 6:11

While Ryan and his father were traveling across the country on
Route 66, they stopped in an unfamiliar small town for some gas. As
the gas station attendant filled the tank, Ryan's dad asked him, "Any
great men or women born in this town?" The attendant replied,
"No, sir, no men and women, just babies."

As the saying goes, great men and women are not born; they are
made—shaped over time by the daily choices they make and the
experiences they have. While the Christian can rightly claim that
everything good we have is thanks to God's abundant grace, this is
not an excuse for passivity. The Christian life is active. "If any man
would come after me," Jesus said, "let him deny himself and take up
his cross and follow me" (Mk 8:34). What does that involve? Jesus
gave many examples: feeding sheep (Jn 21:15–17), turning the other
cheek (Mt 5:39), and loving enemies (Mt 5:44), to name a few. As
Saint Peter explained, you are to "make every effort to supplement
your faith with virtue, and virtue with knowledge, and knowledge
with self-control, and self-control with steadfastness, and steadfastness with godliness, and godliness with brotherly affection, and
brotherly affection with love" (2 Pt 1:5–7). If taken seriously, following Jesus is hardly passive.

Faith and Action

Of the many false dichotomies in the world, the two that are perhaps the most destructive to Christianity are the dichotomy between
faith and action, as if they were two unrelated movements of the
heart, and the dichotomy between grace and nature, as if they were
two independent spheres. As we have stated before, grace builds on
our nature and perfects it. How? By our participation in the life of
God. "His own divine power has granted to us all things that pertain to life and godliness, through the knowledge of him who called
us to his own glory and excellence, by which he has granted to us
his precious and very great promises, that through these you may
escape from the corruption that is in the world because of passion,
and become partakers of the divine nature" (2 Pt 1:3–4). Did you
catch that? We are to become "partakers of the divine nature", and
for that we need both faith and action.

Our first chapter called attention to the fact that we have forgotten
who we are and, as a result, often feel unequipped to grow into the
people God intends us to be. Forgetting is one of the biggest missteps
made by God's people in the Old Testament, for when they forgot
the great things God had done for them, they disobeyed His commandments (see Ex 32:1–35). This is why God instituted the Passover
feast as a perpetual memorial—to remind His people every year of
who they are and what He had done to deliver them from bondage
(see Ex 12:14).

Jesus came not only to remind us of the Passover but to be the
Passover, to reconcile us to God through His sacrifice on the cross.
Therefore, the early Christians called the Eucharist an *anamnesis*, a
Greek word meaning "remembering". The early Church understood
its mission as a continuation of the ministry of Christ to reconcile
God and man. And what is our identity after we are reconciled with
the Father? "See what love the Father has given us, that we should be
called children of God; and so we are" (1 Jn 3:1).

You do not have to be a statistician to know that nearly 100 percent of people want to improve some aspect of their life, to overcome
some unhealthy habit, to become more capable in a particular area,
and so on. This is true of five-year-olds and ninety-five-year-olds.
The desire for improvement is a natural human longing. Deep down,

we want more out of life. We desire more freedom to be ourselves, and we long for more peace. Many people do not know it, but we crave more of God.

The good news is that our heavenly Father wants more of these things for us too. That doesn't mean God will make us rich and famous or give us an easy life. The road that leads to eternal life is hard, Jesus said, but He assured us that His "yoke is easy" and His "burden is light" (Mt 7:14; 11:30). That's because He is carrying the load with us.

The New Testament is full of examples of the difficulties in this world (and Christians, by the way, aren't the only ones who must endure them). What God wants for us is what any good father wants for His children: He wants us to persevere through our trials and tribulations and to develop our character in the process. "Through him we have obtained access to this grace in which we stand, and we rejoice in our hope of sharing the glory of God. More than that, we rejoice in our sufferings, knowing that suffering produces endurance, and endurance produces character, and character produces hope, and hope does not disappoint us" (Rom 5:2–5).

To develop the character God wants for us, it helps to remember the words of Saint Ignatius: "Pray as though everything depended on God. Work as though everything depended on you."[1] We prefer our revised version: "Pray, trusting that God wants the best for you, and take ownership of the mission He has given you." God works through our efforts and often in unexpected ways! God even works through our failures and misfortunes too.

Once there was a man who was shipwrecked on a deserted, uncharted island. He built a crude hut to protect himself and his few remaining possessions and foraged for food as best he could. One day while he was out fishing, his hut was hit by lightning and burst into flames. With no way to put out the fire, the castaway was left with nothing but ashes. He yelled at God, "How could you let this happen to me! Now I've lost everything!" After he calmed down, he realized that he needed God more than ever before, and he repented. He then surrendered himself completely to God. Hours later, a ship came by and sent a rescue team to his island. Once aboard the ship he asked, "How did you know I was here?" The captain replied, "We saw your smoke signal!" Thus,

God is at work even through our trials and the difficult experiences that we don't understand.

When we experience shipwrecks and lightning bolts, many well-intentioned Christians seem to suggest that simply by praying more our problems will go away. While praying is always a good idea in a crisis, and a great source of wisdom, peace, and strength, we also need to put our heads and hands to work, while trusting that God is providing for us through ordinary means even if we do not understand how. No matter the circumstances, we must not lose our confidence in God's provision, which often comes in ways we might not expect. Conversely, the solution to the challenges we face is not *just* more action either. Action without prayer is arrogance. It seeks a solution without realizing that everything comes from God, including our ingenuity and elbow grease. But sometimes it's not until our resources are utterly spent, as when the man's hut went up in smoke, that we finally turn to God.

Action without purpose is another mistake to avoid. Pointless work is drudgery, and we were not made for drudgery but for participation in the creative work of God. After God made man in His own image, He "put him in the garden of Eden to till it and keep it" (Gen 2:15), in other words, to participate in God's work of bringing the garden to fruition. The Fall of Adam and Eve made work harder for themselves and us, but it did not rob work of its meaning. As Saint John Paul II wrote:

> Work is a good thing for man—a good thing for his humanity—because through work man *not only transforms nature*, adapting it to his own needs, but he also *achieves fulfilment* as a human being and indeed, in a sense, becomes "more a human being".
>
> Without this consideration it is impossible to understand the meaning of the virtue of industriousness, and more particularly it is impossible to understand why industriousness should be a virtue: for virtue, as a moral habit, is something whereby man becomes good as man.[2]

It has been said, "Action without prayer is arrogance, and prayer without action is hypocrisy." Most Christians know that they must pray and work. After all, Saint Paul urged us to "pray constantly" (1 Thess 5:17), but he also said, "If any one will not work, let him not eat" (2 Thess 3:10). These two statements do not contradict each other, rather they complement each other. We need both prayer and action to run the race before us and to persevere to the finish line, which is the glory God has prepared for His children from the beginning.

The Battle

Making it to the finish line is going to be a battle—between remembering we are children of God on our way to becoming the Christlike people we are meant to be versus forgetting who we are and refusing to become like Christ. Adam and Eve fell because they forgot who they were. The devil tempted them by saying they could be equal to God by disobeying Him. In their pride, they believed this lie and ate the forbidden fruit. Jesus, the new Adam, through His humility and obedience to the Father, restored our relationship with God and our identity as His children.

Thus, the battle is between *anamnesis*, which is "remembering", and *amnesia*, which is "forgetting". Sometimes God blesses us with a personal awakening, in which we suddenly recognize the truth about ourselves. That's what happened to Tom on a married men's retreat in the desert of Arizona in 1997. He had been so busy with his own goals that he had forgotten that the greatest commandment is to love God and others. By taking some time away from his daily routine, he was able to discern God's will for his life: downsize and simplify so that the truly important things come first.

The battle for each person's soul is part of the war between good and evil, between God and the devil, which rages around us and in us. The genius of the Devil is to convince the world he doesn't exist. "Very few people believe in the devil these days", wrote Bishop Fulton Sheen. "He is always helping to circulate the news of his own death."[3] According to one study, 59 percent of Americans do not believe that the devil is real, but that he is merely the representation of evil.[4] But to defeat our enemy, we must first know that our enemy exists and that his goal is to destroy us! This is not some fairy tale meant to scare us; it is the truth, and it should inspire us to fight back.

While the war is *supernatural* (see Eph 6:12), the battleground is primarily *natural*. This is vitally important to understand. We can fight on the winning side of this war only if we renew our minds, transform our wills, and use our bodies to glorify God. Saint Paul drew a distinction between those who live according to the flesh, meaning the passions and the appetites that lead to sin (such as anger, lust, greed, etc.) and those who live according to the Spirit of God. He wrote, "If you live according to the flesh you will die, but if by the Spirit you put to death the deeds of the body you will live. For all who are led by the Spirit of God are sons of God" (Rom 8:13–14). The war against evil is fought on many fronts, spiritual and physical. Saint Syncletica, a fourth-century Desert Mother who lived as a hermit in Egypt, explained, "Our body is like armor, our soul like the warrior. Take care of both and you will be ready for what comes."[5]

The battle between good and evil begins in the human heart. Consider these words from John R. Wood, a Catholic eye doctor and author of inspirational books: "The war we fight takes place inside the human heart, and it is a battle of the wills. No force on earth and none in hell can take our will from us. Our will is ours. We choose our happiness, and we choose our misery.... We must focus on winning the war inside our hearts—the war between good and evil—and the time is scarce."[6]

To win the war inside our hearts, we first must learn to control our thoughts, for these guide our feelings and ultimately our actions. Simply put, how we think about ourselves and the world around us determines what we choose to do. The popular evangelist and best-selling author Joyce Meyer has written about the battle for our thoughts. We often believe lies about ourselves, about others, and about God, she warns, therefore "we have to think about what we are thinking about because as we think we will become."[7] Test this hypothesis. Have you ever stressed yourself out just by thinking? Have you ever begun to assess a situation and soon found yourself fixated on all the potential problems, convinced that they will lead to imminent ruin? Meanwhile, your heart rate has increased and your blood pressure has gone up. Truly our thoughts impact how we feel, emotionally and physically, which strongly influences how we choose to act.

The devil tells us lies in order to control our thoughts and steer us toward sin. God, on the other hand, tells us the truth, which frees us to see and to choose the good. "There are thousands upon thousands of thoughts presented to us every day", says Meyer. "The mind has to be renewed to follow after the Spirit and not the flesh.... We have to purposely choose right thinking ... to be like-minded with God. We need to choose and continue to choose right thoughts."[8] How we fill our mind is one of the most important decisions we make every moment of our lives. "Occupy your mind with good thoughts," wrote Saint Thomas More, "or the enemy will fill them with bad ones."[9] How true this is. If we do not guide our thoughts and think about good things, we will find ourselves thinking about bad things. Saint Evagrius, a fourth-century Desert Father, said that good thoughts come from our interactions with nature and with God. Bad thoughts come from the evil one. He described bad thoughts as little lies that enter our mind and induce us to sin. These lies are usually about actions that fit into one of the following seven categories: pride, lust, greed, envy, gluttony, anger, and sloth. These have traditionally been called the "seven deadly sins" because if they become habits, they can lead to death—physical and spiritual. But don't expect the devil to tell you that; he'll say just the opposite.

When a particular sin becomes a habit, we call it a vice. No sane person wants to be enslaved to a vice. In fact, in the English language to be "vice-filled" is to be *vicious*. We commonly use the word *vicious* to describe animals that are particularly fierce toward human beings. Such animals are not immoral because they do not have free will, but act out of instinct. Not so for a vicious person who has chosen to become a slave to sin. Yet like a rabid dog, he is a danger to himself and others.

Our vices impact our families, friends, and others around us. If you've ever watched the Blue Angels or any other precision flying team, you know that if one jet strays from the disciplined formation even a little bit, all five jets will likely crash into each other. The same is true for us. When we sin, we are like a top that starts spinning out of control and bumping into everything before wobbling and falling over. Our sinful actions cause us to lose control and to harm those closest to us.

In later chapters, we will cover the vices in greater detail as well as the virtues we need to develop in order to overcome them. For now, let us continue to examine the battle to control our thoughts. "Do not be conformed to this world," wrote Saint Paul, "but be transformed by the renewal of your mind, that you may prove what is the will of God, what is good and acceptable and perfect" (Rom 12:2). One way we renew our minds is to enlighten ourselves with the truth.

The Four Forgotten Truths, Revisited

When the devil tempts us, he not only lies about one of the seven deadly sins, saying it's not really bad but actually good, he also lies about God and His amazing plan for each one of us. Look at how he tempted Adam and Eve. He told them that they would not die if they ate from the forbidden tree but would become like God, which was not only untrue but also the same as calling God a liar. If we are going to do battle against the devil's cunning falsehoods, we need to arm ourselves with the truth, including the following four truths that we introduced in chapter 1.

1. God wants us to be happy

God wants nothing more than for us to be happy. Scripture is full of verses about God's goodness and His desire for our well-being. Jesus said, "What father among you, if his son asks for a fish, will instead of a fish give him a serpent; or if he asks for an egg, will give him a scorpion? If you then, who are evil, know how to give good gifts to your children, how much more will the heavenly Father give the Holy Spirit to those who ask him!" (Lk 11:11–13).

We know this to be true. Parents, as imperfect as they may be, want what is best for their children. Often this requires that they direct their children away from evil and toward what is good, knowing better than they do what will really make them happy. Likewise, God knows better than we do what will make us truly happy, and He gives us commandments to guide us in the right direction. As fathers we have learned that when our children fall, we are not angry as much as we are sad that they chose to settle for something that will neither help them nor fulfill them in the long run. If we, as imperfect fathers, feel this way, how much more does our heavenly Father desire the best for us.

From time to time, we set our hearts on things that, even if they are good, won't provide lasting happiness. This is especially easy to do in our consumeristic society, where we associate buying and having stuff with happiness. We can all think of times when we thought that having a particular thing—a new car or a new phone—would make us happy. We experienced a certain thrill at first, but then it wore off, and we found ourselves wanting something else.

When Ryan was a young boy there was a contest for a new red motocross bike with twenty-inch chrome rims. While he didn't win the raffle, he was sure that this bike would be the source of ultimate happiness and said as much to his father. On his birthday a few weeks later, his father gave him the bike with a ribbon on it! He was so excited and so happy as he cruised down the street—that is, until about three minutes and thirty-eight seconds later, when another kid passed by on a new twenty-four-inch chrome cruiser bicycle. Ryan felt that he had made a horrible mistake. He ran home and told his dad, "This bike won't make me happy. I need a twenty-four-inch chrome cruiser to make me truly happy."

Our fallen nature always leaves us wanting more and more stuff or bigger and better stuff to try filling that God-shaped hole in our hearts. Tom was a successful national advertising executive for over twenty years, and he can tell you that the advertising industry invests billions of dollars to entice us to buy more and more stuff in a futile attempt to fill a void that can be filled only by God Himself.

We make the same futile attempt to fill the God-shaped hole with our other wants, whether for pleasure or recognition. We tend to be complacent about our spiritual life while indulging these desires, as though we really don't believe that communion with God is the ultimate happiness. C. S. Lewis explained this very well: "It would seem that Our Lord finds our desires not too strong, but too weak. We are half-hearted creatures, fooling about with drink and sex and ambition when infinite joy is offered us, like an ignorant child who wants to go on making mud pies in a slum because he cannot imagine what is meant by the offer of a holiday at the sea. We are far too easily pleased."[10]

For ancient Greeks and Romans, the three goals of the good life were pleasure, honor, and power. Are we any different today? Some of the Greek philosophers and, later, the Christians and the Roman Stoics saw this vision of the good life as flawed and superficial. In his book *Finding True Happiness*, Father Robert Spitzer, S.J., provides a witty and thoughtful review of the Greek philosophers on this subject.[11] He explains that they considered happiness as the one thing that we will for itself because everything we do is for the purpose of making us happy. He also explains that there are four levels to happiness, and that God created us to be fully satisfied by nothing less than the top level. This is the reason why we are often disappointed when things we thought would make us happy, don't—at least not for long.

According to Father Spitzer, the first level of happiness is *laetus*, from the Latin word meaning "delighted". This level of happiness usually comes from the senses, which register the physical pleasure we experience while enjoying, for example, a good meal after a long day or a strong cup of coffee in the morning. These are not necessarily bad things, but they are insufficient to make us completely happy and leave us wanting more.

The second level of happiness is *felix*, from the Latin word for "lucky" or "fortunate". This second level lasts a little longer because it involves more than just the physical senses. It comes from being esteemed, honored, and liked by others. But this too has limits. A charismatic liar may be liked by many people, but he is not fulfilled. An honest person may not be esteemed by others, but he is ultimately happier than a dishonest person, proving that there is more to happiness than just *felix*.

While the first two levels of happiness are directed inward toward our physical and emotional feelings, the third and fourth levels of happiness are directed outward toward others and, ultimately, God. The third level of happiness, *beatitudo*, points to the service and love of others. It is deeply satisfying and longer-lasting than the first two levels. The fourth level of happinesss, *sublimitas*, points to the service and love of God. It is the happiness that comes from being in right relationship with God, from fulfilling the demands of the Gospel, from forgiving others and being forgiven, and from having an epiphany or an experience of profound peace. *Sublimitas* is hard to put into words, but it is the profound happiness that we all are ultimately seeking. As Saint Augustine said, "You have made me for yourself, O Lord, and my heart is restless until it rests in you."[12] The top two levels of happiness call to mind the words of Christ: "You shall love the Lord your God with all your heart, and with all your soul, and with all your mind. This is the great and first commandment. And a second is like it, You shall love your neighbor as yourself. On these two commandments depend all the law and the prophets" (Mt 22:36–40). It seems that the greatest commandment is telling us how to be truly happy.

2. The Christian life takes work

Much of the first part of this chapter focused on the need for effort in the Christian life. Following Christ is not passive or boring; it is active and dynamic. We must respond to the challenges we face with both prayer and work, while accepting God's grace as His beloved sons and daughters. At the end of our lives we want to hear: "Well done, good and faithful servant ... enter into the joy of your master" (Mt 25:21). Who is the faithful servant? "Not every one who says to me, 'Lord, Lord,' shall enter the kingdom of heaven," said Jesus, "but he who does the will of my Father who is in heaven" (Mt 7:21). And what is the will of God? "For this is the will of God," wrote Saint Paul, "your sanctification" (1 Thess 4:3). In other words, God wants you to be holy, and He knows that your being holy is what will lead to your happiness and fulfillment.

The basic Christian message can be summarized as follows: First, we are sinners and can't save ourselves. Second, God comes to save us through the atoning sacrifice of Christ on the cross, which frees us from sin and reconciles us to God. Third, God offers us the gift of eternal life, which we must accept and make operative in our lives. As Saint Augustine said, "God created us without us: but he did not will to save us without us."[13] Our consent to being saved by God, to having our wills conformed to His will with the help of His grace, is our work. It is our life's project. Just as everyone is called to participate in God's work of creation, everyone is called to participate in His work of salvation. This not a secret or some new knowledge; this is the foundation of the Christian life.

The Benedictine motto of *ora et labora* (pray and work) sums up the Christian life. Saint Benedict and his followers knew who they were and what they needed to do to become who they were called to be. And their way of life preserved and eventually renewed Western culture in the Middle Ages. Christian prayer and work can renew society again today, starting with ourselves.

3. Grace builds upon nature

When God saw everything He made, He said it was "very good" (Gen 1: 31). We are to discover in creation the goodness and the love of God and the truth about ourselves.

> *Nature expresses a design of love and truth.* It is prior to us, and it has been given to us by God as the setting for our life. Nature speaks to us of the Creator (cf. Rom 1:20) and his love for humanity.... Nature is at our disposal not as "a heap of scattered refuse", but as a gift of the Creator who has given it an inbuilt order, enabling man to draw from it the principles needed in order "to till it and keep it" (Gen 2:15).[14]

Yes, the Fall of Adam and Eve ushered sin and death into the world and distorted our relationship with nature. But God did not leave mankind and the world He created to perish. Rather, He entered the world, by taking on human flesh, in order to redeem us and make us like Himself by sharing His divine nature with us. "For he was made man that we might be made God."[15] And man is not the only one to be transformed. "According to his promise we wait for new heavens and a new earth in which righteousness dwells" (2 Pet 3:13). For this reason, Saint Paul wrote, "I consider that the sufferings of this present time are not worth comparing with the glory that is to be revealed to us. For the creation waits with eager longing for the revealing of the sons of God.... We know that the whole creation has been groaning with labor pains together until now; and not only the creation, but we ourselves" (Rom 8:18–23).

What is the raw material that God uses to take us sinners and make us into sons and daughters like Himself? Ourselves, as we are. Our transformation in Christ doesn't destroy nature but turns it into what it was always meant to be. When the serpent lied to Adam and Eve, telling them that eating the forbidden fruit would make them like God, he was in fact saying a partial truth. The Fall is what made our redemption and sanctification necessary and possible, as the Church exclaims at the Easter Vigil: "O truly necessary sin of Adam, destroyed completely by the Death of Christ! O happy fault that earned so great, so glorious a Redeemer!"[16]

In C. S. Lewis' fable *The Great Divorce*, there is a man who has died and is walking toward heaven with a small red lizard on his shoulder. The red lizard represents one of the seven deadly sins, most likely lust. The lizard is whispering in his ear half-truths and sowing doubt, which is hindering the man's progress. The man must decide either to listen to the lizard or to be rid of that nagging voice forever. Through the intervention of an angel, the man finally parts from the lizard. To the man's surprise, the lizard does not die but is transformed into a beautiful stallion, which carries him the rest of the way to heaven.

C. S. Lewis is showing that sin distorts our nature and diminishes its goodness. For example, our desire for sexual union is not bad, but good because God created it as part of human nature. But if this desire becomes merely an appetite for pleasure apart from and contrary to the purposes of marriage, it is distorted into lust—a small, selfish, and ugly sin. Growing in virtue is not about suppressing our desires as much as it is about controlling and directing them toward what is truly good for us.

4. We were never meant to go through life alone

Listen well, as this may be the most important thing you hear all day, all week, all year, maybe in your entire adult life. Ready? *You cannot do it alone.* We do not just mean that you can't do it without God, we mean that you can't do it without the help of others as well. We are made for communion. A child can live longer without food or water than it can without human affection. This phenomenon was observed in the orphanages of war-torn Europe. In newborn intensive care units, nurses have timers that remind them to touch and talk to the babies. Babies need human contact and love, and so do we. God made us this way, and that is a great thing.

We can't succeed in this life without help. We need to live in communion not only with God but with others who share our faith in Him. We need friends and relatives who can encourage us when we are struggling. And we in turn need to encourage them, as the oft-quoted saying advises: "Be kind, for everyone is fighting a hard battle."[17] Even when we must enter the battle or the challenge alone, we are joined in spirit by our friends both here and in heaven, who pray for us. The fact is, we are never alone. God is with us always.

God is always speaking to us through His creation, His word, and our circumstances in life. He gives us His grace in prayer and in the sacraments of the Church. He helps us through the example and the intercession of the saints, those capital "S" saints and those lower case "saints" like our grandparents or others we may know who lived exemplary Christian lives. Also, God helps us through our family members and friends who share and support our faith. It is important to have relationships with people who know who you are, challenge you to become the person God created you to be, and fight the good fight alongside you. Unfortunately, in this fallen world there are a thousand voices that will cheer you to your ruin, but only a few that will challenge you to become better.

The battle is real, and the battle is now. God says, "I have set before you this day life and good, death and evil. If you obey the commandments of the LORD your God which I command you this day, by loving the LORD your God, by walking in his ways, and by keeping his commandments and his statutes and his ordinances, then you shall live and multiply, and the LORD your God will bless you in the land which you are entering to take possession of it" (Deut 30:15–16). The land we are entering is eternal life with God, and the journey and the struggle to arrive there starts today.

3

Knowing Yourself

"You knitted me together in my mother's womb.
I praise you, for I am wondrously made."

—Psalm 139:13–14

Jesus taught in parables, short moral stories that contain a rule or an observation from life about the way things are or ought to be. Parables illustrate the obvious-but-forgotten truths about who we are and why we are here. They point us toward our true home, the Kingdom of God. The Parable of the Prodigal Son (Lk 15:11–32) reveals God's incredible, compassionate paternal love for His children. The Good Samaritan (Lk 10:25–37) shows us our duty to care for and love others. The Laborers in the Vineyard (Mt 20) teaches us about the generosity of God and our reliance on Him.

Let's look more closely at one parable in particular. Jesus said, "The kingdom of heaven is like a grain of mustard seed which a man took and sowed in his field; it is the smallest of all seeds, but when it has grown it is the greatest of shrubs and becomes a tree, so that the birds of the air come and make nests in its branches" (Mt 13:31–32). It is true that the mustard seed is remarkably small, yet in the deserts of the Holy Land, a mustard tree (think of a very large bush) stands out and provides cover for other plants to grow and shelter for wildlife. Though small in its beginning, the mustard seed plays an important role in God's design. We both have lived in Phoenix, Arizona, and we understand the benefit of shade in the desert. When the temperature is 115 degrees or higher, it's no joke to pray fervently for the rare shady parking place.

God's Plan for Us

Our lives are much the same as the mustard seed—seemingly small, insignificant, and temporary yet destined by God for greater things than we can imagine. And unlike mustard seeds, we have an intellect and a will; we can choose to cooperate with God's plan. And when we do, we not only grow and flourish but help others to grow and flourish too. With the mustard seed, Jesus used an image that the people of the time knew and recognized to explain a forgotten truth—that in God's hands, even small things play important roles.

Here is another parable. We are like travelers who know their destination and begin their journey despite not knowing all the details of the trip. Many great stories are about a person who embarks on a journey or a quest but does not entirely know the way. The hero's success is partly dependent on his personal growth and partly the result of outside help, or put another way, divine intervention. Think of *The Odyssey, The Lord of the Rings, The Wizard of Oz*, and even *Star Wars*. While the characters, the settings, and the adventures are all very different, the basic plot involves the many challenges the hero encounters in order to become the person he was meant to be.

An old adage says, "If you want to make God laugh, tell Him your plans." In each of these stories, and in our lives too, the main character starts out knowing very little about the person he is destined to become. He has plans of his own that are based on his very limited ideas about himself. He expands only as he attempts to do what is asked of him along the way. As Pope Benedict XVI said, "Man was created for greatness—for God Himself; he was created to be filled by God. But his heart is too small for the greatness to which it is destined. It must be stretched."[1] The point is this: we come to know and to become our true selves by staying faithful to the mission God gives us, with all of its conspiracies of graces.

From a Christian perspective, the great journey of life is to become the person God has created you to be, which is also the only way to find true and everlasting happiness. We become that person by cooperating with His grace as we face challenges along the path He gives us. God loves us too much to let us settle for our own limited ideas of ourselves and remain in our comfort zones. That's why He planted within us the big questions.

The Big Questions

Developmental psychology tells us that we all ask ourselves key questions at particular times during our physical, emotional, and psychological development. From a very young age we begin to ask, "Where did I come from?" This question of our origin may at first stem from curiosity about the natural world, as when a young child asks his blushing parents where babies come from in front of a dinner guest! The next question usually emerges in adolescence: "Why am I here?" This is a question of purpose, and it is often prompted by the longings of one's heart. It is deeply connected to what we do in life in order to pursue the things that we believe will make us happy. As we mature and become more introspective, we ask: "Where am I going?" This question of destination can be practical and short-term. "Where am I going to go to college?" "Where am I going to live when my parents finally kick me out of the house?" But it can also be big and ultimate, like "What is my destiny in life?" or "What happens when I die?"

These questions of origin, purpose, and destiny are related to the deepest question of the human heart: "Who am I?" Figuring out who we are is one of life's great challenges. We tend to equate our identity with our job, political affiliation, ethnicity, gender, age bracket, income level, and so on, but it is much more profound than all of these things put together. To tackle this question, let's take each of the other questions one at a time.

Where did I come from?

On the question of origin, we can say with accuracy that we are the result of the fusion of equally contributing DNA from both of our parents that occurred at the moment of our conception. The more we learn about the earliest stage of human life, the more we know how intricate and complicated it is, pointing us toward the reality of a Creator. But however amazing the natural process that brought us into being is, it answers only the question of our biological origin. It doesn't answer why there is life in the first place or why I am here, which is what we really want to know.

Many people have adopted a materialist view of the world. In other words, they believe that matter is all there is. For them, there is no God and no human soul; human beings, then, are random, meaningless outcomes of natural processes. Some modern materialists have described us as "matter in motion" (David Hume), "bits of stardust" (Lawrence Krauss), and "gene machines" (Richard Dawkins). There is truth to these statements: we are matter in motion; our cell structure is made up of the very atoms that existed and were scattered by the creation of the stars; and yes, we are exceedingly well-designed machines able to perform certain tasks. Yet, we are so much more than that.

We are thinking, choosing, acting, loving beings. Observing these qualities has led many intelligent people throughout the ages to conclude that we are creations of God, who made us in His image (see Gen 1:26). The beauty and the complexity and the ingeniousness of everything that exists suggested to them that there must be a Creator. "The heavens are telling the glory of God; and the firmament proclaims his handiwork" (Ps 19:1). Where did I come from? Why am I here? The short answer is that I and everything else there is came from God. He willed me into being out of pure love. He is the reason I am here.

What is my purpose in life?

Often when people ask why they are here, they mean what is their purpose in life. Just as we first looked at biology to answer the question of our origins, we can also look at biology to address the question of our purpose. After all, a hammer is made the way it is in order to fulfill its purpose of pounding nails.

On a basic level we have certain immediate needs and the equipment, so to speak, to go about meeting them, which can provide some sense of our purpose. We need enough food, water, and shelter to survive. We are also sexual beings, created male and female, and we participate in the generation of new life through the sexual union of a man and woman. We can even go further and say that due to our complexity and slow maturation rate, humans need more guidance, protection, and nourishment from their parents than other animals. Related to this, they flourish best with the stability that is provided by having their mother and their father in a permanent, committed relationship.

Although food, water, and home are important to our lives, they are all means to an end and therefore do not constitute our ultimate purpose. We are more than just eating, more than just ensuring the continuation of our species. We have particular talents and gifts that can benefit others, and we can share life together in ways that build each other up. We don't need to have religious faith to appreciate our social nature and to see that using our gifts to provide for ourselves and serve others brings happiness. Secular organizations grant big awards to honor those who make significant contributions to arts, science, and diplomacy. In addition to our natural gifts, we receive spiritual gifts from God, which Saint Paul said are for the sake of the whole Church: "Now there are varieties of gifts, but the same Spirit; and there are varieties of service, but the same Lord; and there are varieties of working, but it is the same God who inspires them all in every one. To each is given the manifestation of the Spirit for the common good" (1 Cor 12:4–7). Thus, our gifts and abilities do reveal something about our purpose. Yet we have an even deeper, transcendent purpose, which our biology and our social nature point toward.

Some say that we have no other purpose than our own survival and that of the species. According to this belief, everything we do serves either ourselves or our tribe. As we come to think of ourselves as self-sufficient and to see the group as unimportant to our survival, this view takes on an exaggerated self-centeredness. From this perspective, there is no such thing as disinterested love. Even the heroic act of someone giving up his life to save another person is seen as behavior that evolved in order to perpetuate the human race.

Others believe that we are made for the lowest level of happiness, *laetus*, which we discussed in chapter 2. Nothing new about this idea. Our word "hedonist" comes from the Greek word *hedon*, which means "pleasure". For the ancient Greek hedonists, and those who have followed in their footsteps, our purpose is to maximize pleasure and to minimize the experience of pain. In this philosophy, "If it feels good, do it; if it feels bad, run away." Taken to an extreme, that could mean eating ice cream for dinner and never going to the dentist. Reasonable people realize that too many sweets are harmful to one's health and that some pain is necessary in order to avoid worse evils. However, that doesn't stop people from acting as though maximizing comfort were the main goal of life.

But it's not the main goal of life. "Why did God make you?" was one of the first questions in the *Baltimore Catechism*. The answer: "God made me to know Him, to love Him, and to serve Him in this world, and to be happy with Him forever in the next."² The truth is, it's not up to us to determine our purpose. It's been given to us by our Creator and should be the reason for every choice we make. Before we make a decision we should ask ourselves: Which course of action will help me to know, to love, and to serve God?

In a society that prizes the person who "goes for it" and obtains what he wants against all odds, it's not easy to keep our true goal in view. We love the movie *Rudy*, and other films like it, because we all love a good underdog story, where the hero has dreamed a seemingly impossible dream and it comes true because of his determination and effort. But when a five-year-old boy says he wants to be a lion when he grows up, somebody needs to tell him that is not possible. The fact is, we can't be literally anything we want because we don't make ourselves; we are creatures of God. This might sound harsh to some people, but the truth of our lives is far more wonderful than anything we could dream up for ourselves.

God has made us for an epic adventure—becoming the unique and unrepeatable man or woman He created us to be by knowing, loving, and serving Him. His plan unfolds in surprising and amazing ways as He leads us to complete fulfillment and perfect happiness. "For I know the plans I have for you," said the Lord through the prophet Jeremiah, "plans for welfare and not for evil, to give you a future and a hope" (Jer 29:11). Have you ever wondered why God made you to live in this particular time and place? He has a plan for your life. Saint John Henry Newman described the Lord's plan for his life, and ours, this way:

> He has committed some work to me which He has not committed to another. I have my mission—I may never know it in this life, but I shall be told it in the next.... I am a link in a chain, a bond of connection between persons. He has not created me for naught. I shall do good; I shall do His work.... if I do but keep His commandments and serve Him in my calling.... Therefore I will trust Him. Whatever, wherever I am, I can never be thrown away.... He does nothing in vain.... He knows what He is about.³

What is my destiny?

In short, our destiny is eternal happiness with God. As we have shown, our purpose and our destiny are linked together. Becoming the person we were created to be—by knowing, loving, and serving God—is the road to our destination in heaven.

Having an eternal perspective is somewhat rare these days. Many people around us believe that this life is all there is. Death is the end of the road, they think, so squeeze as much pleasure out of life as possible. It is worth noting that thankfully many good people who believe that this world is all there is, nevertheless give generously of themselves to make it a better and more beautiful place. That's because God has made us like Himself and built self-giving into our very nature, as the Second Vatican Council proclaimed and Saint John Paul II regularly reminded us: "This likeness reveals that man, who is the only creature on earth which God willed for itself, cannot fully find himself except through a sincere gift of himself."[4]

Putting It All Together

The entire Christian faith is based on our being created in God's image and likeness, our forgetting who we are and falling into sin, and our being redeemed by a loving Father, so as to live in communion with Him now and forever. As we have seen, participating in God's plan for our lives is what following Jesus is all about. You are already doing this or you wouldn't be reading this book. The point of *The WillPower Advantage* is to help you do this better.

The very first step is to know ourselves better. The general answers to the questions above reveal a lot about ourselves, but there are also personal answers to particular questions that can fill out the picture of ourselves even more. Among these are the following:

1. How has God made me?
   • What is my temperament?
   • What are my talents and personal interests?
2. How have my experiences shaped who I am?
   • What blessings have been given to me?
   • What wounds do I still carry from childhood and beyond that affect me today?
3. What is my particular purpose in life? What is the mission God has given me?

4. What must I do to answer God's unique calling for me, to fulfill that mission?
5. What are the weaknesses that hinder me from doing that?

Intellect, Will, and Appetite

Let's look at the last question first. But before we do, let's try to understand a bit better how our weaknesses get the upper hand. Saint Paul has described our situation perfectly: "For I do not do the good I want, but the evil I do not want is what I do" (Rom 7:19). Paul is not talking about genuine mistakes, accidents, or misjudgments; he means sin—the intentional commission of an action that he knows is wrong or omission of an action that he knows he ought to do. The truth is, we all sin, but we should try not to sin.

It's hard work not to sin, especially when certain sins have become habits. Have you ever sat there on New Year's Eve saying to yourself, "Aren't these the same New Year's resolutions that I made last year? Gee, what happened?" Or perhaps you find yourself confessing the same sins over and over again. While it's true that most of us battle the same weaknesses throughout our lives, it's not true that there is nothing we can do to improve. But the first step is knowing the three components involved in the choices we make. These are commonly called the intellect, the will, and the appetite.

The intellect is that part of us that thinks and rationalizes, the will is that part of us that moves us to action, and the appetite is that part of us that desires and pulls us toward things. It may be helpful to think of intellect as *what I know*, will as *what I do*, and appetite as *what I want*. All three interact in important ways. What is most important to know is that our intellect cannot on its own move us toward what is good. I can know that eating a whole carton of ice cream for dinner is not good, but that knowledge does not, on its own, keep the spoon from expertly moving the creamy treat from the carton to my mouth, over and over again. Why? Because our actions are not just dependent on knowledge, though knowledge plays an important role, rather they are dependent primarily on our will, how we choose to act, which can be more strongly influenced by our appetite than by our intellect.

The Teeter-Totter

Think of a teeter-totter, the fun and somewhat dangerous playground equipment from our youth. With children of equal weight and strength, the teeter-totter is balanced, where a push by one child's feet sends him up while the other child goes down and vice-versa. However, if one child is slightly bigger and stronger, he sends the smaller child flying as he crashes to the ground.

Now imagine a virtual teeter-totter of intellect versus appetite. Since what we desire is always more than necessary, our appetite is the larger kid, while our intellect is the smaller one. The result? The appetite will dominate, and the intellect will be taken for a rough ride. There is a solution: equal out the weight. If the will is added to the intellect, they can govern the appetite and direct it toward the good.

When the will is aligned to the appetite, they suppress the intellect. Plato, the ancient Greek philosopher, said that when this happens a person becomes a "monster". We would not use this word today, but we do have a name for people who have so aligned their wills with their appetites that they are incapable of rational decision making. We call them "addicts", whether they are addicted to drugs, alcohol, sex, food, gambling, or anything else. Some of us are addicts in the clinical sense, and we need help to re-form our wills to align with our intellects, so that we can control and direct our desires or appetites toward what is good for us.

If you suffer from an addiction, you are not alone. Please seek professional help. This book can help provide a strong framework for understanding the challenges you face, but it cannot replace the help that is provided by a professional or twelve-step program. God wants us free from our addictions because they keep us enslaved and hinder us from knowing and becoming who we really are.

While not all of us are addicts, all of us have allowed our will to become dominated by our appetite to some degree, which has diminished our intellect's ability to guide our appetite toward what we know is best for us. So we all have some work to do, to align our will with our intellect so that we can choose the good and become the person God wants us to be. This work involves acquiring virtues, which are the habits of doing good that we will examine in detail in the second part of this book. When we cultivate virtues, our appetite is not suppressed, it is not made small and weak. Rather it is liberated, made free to want what will truly make us happy and to reject those things that steal our peace and rob our joy.

Think about it, there is no *AppetitePower Advantage*, because there is no real advantage to growing your appetite. Such a book, if it were honest, would carry a surgeon general's health warning. There is also no *IntellectualPower Advantage*, because just forming the intellect is not enough. In fact, being smart and capable with a poorly formed will can be a dangerous thing indeed. The advantage of forming the will is clear. Form the will well, through acquiring good habits, and what you want becomes focused on the things you truly desire and will lead to lasting happiness. And as a bonus, your intellect grows wiser in the process. This is the goal of *WillPower Advantage*.

The Heart

The interaction of these three components—the intellect, the will, and the appetite—direct and form the heart, *what I love*. We often think of the heart as the inmost being of a person, and it is. The heart is where we feel the effects of our thoughts, desires, and decisions. Forming our intellect and will well naturally forms our heart well, and we learn to love the things that God loves, and dream the dreams that God has for us.

We begin our formation with the following advice from Saint Paul: "Whatever is true, whatever is honorable, whatever is just, whatever is pure, whatever is lovely, whatever is gracious, if there is any excellence, if there is anything worthy of praise, think about these things" (Phil 4:8). And it continues with building habits of doing good, or virtues, which bring real and lasting happiness.

Knowing that your intellect, will, and appetite work together within your heart is important. And it is also important to know the particular ways in which you see and respond to the world. Your perceptions and responses are related to the temperament that God has given you. There are four basic temperaments, which we now will explain.

The Four Temperaments

Think of all the comedies based on a person who suddenly experiences amnesia. After a series of hilarious events, in which the person learns some valuable lessons, the person suddenly remembers who he is. Imagine for a moment that you woke up with no idea of who you are. What questions would you ask? "Am I married?" "Do I have any children?" "How old am I?" "Where do I live?" You might even ask: "What type of person am I?" Meaning, am I typically happy or sad, deep or light-hearted, introverted or extroverted, and so on. These traits make up our temperament.

Our temperament is the result of both biology and environment. It is made up of the default tendencies that come naturally to a person. Art and Laraine Bennett, in their excellent book _The Temperament God Gave You_, explain temperament as "the sum of our natural preferences; it shapes our thoughts, ideas, impressions, and the way we tend to react to our environment and to other people." It is "our predisposition to react in certain ways".[5]

A long time ago, the father of medicine, Hippocrates, described four general temperaments, which he called the four "humors". He believed that fluids in the body affected emotion and attitude. While modern medicine would disagree with Hippocrates about the fluids, modern psychology continues to use the four temperaments to identify traits that people tend to have. The four temperaments are choleric, sanguine, melancholic, and phlegmatic. In brief, cholerics are people of action motivated by results, sanguines are people persons motivated by relationships, melancholics are deep-thinking people motivated by ideas, and phlegmatics are diplomatic people motivated by keeping the peace. Generally, each of us strongly possesses one of these temperaments and more moderately manifests a second temperament.

Here is a question to help clarify. How would you react if you arrived at a party that was a flop? If you would take charge, identify the problems, and reorganize the party, you are likely _choleric_. If you would introduce people to each other and gather people around the piano for a sing-along, you are likely _sanguine_. If you would sit down to analyze the possibilities that could have led to such a party, you are likely _melancholic_. If you would find the host to discuss what has happened and to make sure that no one's feelings have been hurt, you are likely *phlegmatic*.

Another gauge of temperament, developed by Alexandre Havard, is how quickly or slowly a person reacts and how long he can persist. Cholerics tend to be quick in reacting and have a lot of energy to persist. Sanguines tend to be quick in reacting but short on the ability to stay the course. Melancholics tend to be slow in reacting but have a lot of energy to persist. Phlegmatics tend to be slow in reacting and short on the ability to stay the course. For this reason, you cannot have both a choleric and a phlegmatic temperament or both a sanguine and a melancholic temperament.

It is important to remember that you are not just your temperament. Your temperament is a part of who you are. As Havard explains, "It is the foundation upon which we build our character."[6] It is also the basis of your personality. That's why knowing your temperament is very helpful for knowing and understanding yourself, which is the first step in identifying the areas where you need to grow. In the next chapter, you will learn to identify your temperament by taking The Spiritual Audit, and then you will be on your way to becoming the person God created you to be.

4

The Spiritual Audit

"I am sure that he who began a good work in you will bring it to completion."

— Philippians 1:6

The first three chapters of this book set the foundation for the real work that lies ahead. We discussed the central problem: we need to follow Jesus more closely to become the person we are meant to be. We discussed the challenge: remembering who we are as beloved sons and daughters of God and living accordingly. We introduced the solution: growing in virtue with the help of God's grace. And finally, we introduced the idea that growing in virtue is primarily about forming your will so that it conforms to God's will for you, which leads to true and lasting happiness. We also introduced the importance of knowing yourself in order to understand where you need to begin. The previously mentioned saying "Know thyself, and thy faults, and thus live", commonly attributed to Saint Augustine, drives home the important work of knowing yourself, which is what The Spiritual Audit will help you to do.

Much of the first three chapters was a basic review of Christian teaching. Most of us need a refresher course; we sure did. For years we thought that becoming holy, or growing in virtue, was just about praying more or working harder. And we found ourselves in a rut. Here is the good news: you can get out of that rut by participating in God's plan for you—His specific plan concerning how He made you and what He made you for. This requires knowing a lot about yourself, beginning with your temperament and personality.

Consider the temperament and personality differences among the apostles. Peter was impulsive, always speaking without quite understanding things (see Matt 16:22–23). James and John were ambitious mama's boys (see Matt 20:20–23). Paul, formerly Saul, was self-righteous and hot-tempered. Before his life-changing encounter with the risen Christ, he was so zealous for his Jewish faith that he was "breathing threats and murder against the disciples of the Lord" (Acts 9:1). In each of these cases, conversion and transformation in Christ did not change the person's temperament. Rather, the grace of God perfected each temperament and directed it toward communion with Him. By grace building on the foundation of his temperament, Peter became the contrite, docile, and steadfast disciple that Jesus chose to be the leader of the Church (Mt 16:18). James and John became bold witnesses and pillars of faith (Gal 2:9), and Paul lost nothing of his fiery zeal, but used it to win souls for Christ (see 2 Cor 11: 23–28). See where we are going?

God does not want to destroy you or make you into someone or something you are not. No, He wants to transform you and mold you into who you truly are. Remember His words and call them to mind often: "For I know the plans I have for you, says the LORD, plans for welfare and not for evil, to give you a future and a hope" (Jer 29:11). God loves you just as you are, yet way too much to leave you that way. He is calling each of us to conversion and transformation in Christ, to become the people He has created us to be—His beloved sons and daughters!

Consider for a moment how different each of your siblings or other family members are. A college friend of Ryan's met him and his brother separately. Because they were so different from each other, he did not realize they were brothers. When he found out, he exclaimed, "You came out of the same womb?!" Each person is a unique individual, and one of the factors that contributes to his unique personality is his temperament.

There are a lot of different personality-type tests available, and there is a good chance that you have taken an assessment such as Myers-Briggs, StrengthsFinder, DISC, and so on. These tests are good; however, The Spiritual Audit has dimensions that they lack. It is not a personality-type indicator, nor is it a temperament quiz. It is a comprehensive self-examination that includes your temperament, natural strengths and weaknesses, and the virtues you need to develop in order to overcome the temptations and the compulsions that lead you to vice and steal your peace and joy.

The Spiritual Audit can help you to discover how God has made you and to assess how you can more actively participate in His plan to become the person He has created you to be. Set aside an hour to pray and to complete the audit below. Afterward, you can move on to the rest of the book, which focuses on ways you can build on what you have learned about yourself.

THE SPIRITUAL AUDIT

Introduction

This simple assessment is a tool we created with a team of experienced theological professionals, trained psychologists, pastors, and ordinary men and women who want to help you to grow in virtue and become the person God created you to be. You can find more resources to help you, including an online Spiritual Audit workbook, at www.amenalleluia.com.

Awareness of Strengths and Weaknesses

A strength is something that makes you a better person, and a weakness is something that stands in the way of your becoming a better person. Over time and with practice, our strengths can become virtues. Left unchecked, our weaknesses can become vices. With this in mind, answer questions 1–3.

1. How aware are you of your strengths and weaknesses?

Select one of the following:

A. I am very aware of both my strengths and my weaknesses.
B. I am very aware of my weaknesses but still discovering my strengths.
C. I am very aware of my strengths but still discovering my weaknesses.
D. I am still discovering both my strengths and weaknesses.

If you answered A, please continue on to the next question below. If you answered B, C, or D, take a moment to dive a little deeper.

Diving Deeper

Many of us are still discovering our strengths and weaknesses. That is okay, and in reality, it can take a lifetime to learn what all of your strengths and weaknesses are.

Strengths can be things that come naturally to you and, as a result, often do not require a lot of physical or mental energy to acquire. These are the things people might say come easily to you. Sometimes they are the result of a gift you were born with, for example musical aptitude in a person with perfect pitch or athletic ability in a person with excellent eye-hand coordination. Strengths can also be things that you have learned to do well over time through much effort. These things do require a lot of physical and mental energy even if we have a natural aptitude for them. A piano virtuoso might have innate musical ability, but it took years of hard work for her to become one of the best pianists in the world. Even if he's a natural athlete, the golf pro practiced for years to be at the top of his game.

There are also strengths that people acquire without having an inborn gift. Perhaps you know a superb administrator who can manage multiple tasks and people with expert care and efficiency; yet for this person these skills did not come naturally. Rather he worked hard to learn them and exerts significant effort to use them. There are also supernatural strengths, special graces given to us by God that help us to fulfill the mission He has given us. Such abilities have no natural explanation. More typical for the Christian, however, is the grace that allows him to stretch beyond what he thinks are his natural limits. What Saint Paul said about himself is true for all of us: "I can do all things in him who strengthens me" (Phil 4:13).

When we practice a strength, whether natural or developed, it can become a good habit, or virtue. A virtue is a disposition to choose the good, the beautiful, and the true, in other words, the things that make us truly happy.

Like strengths, weaknesses can arise from inborn tendencies, and some of these are related to our temperament. Cholerics, for example, are prone to speaking before thinking because they are action-oriented. Sanguines are prone to being overly optimistic because they want to make themselves and others happy. Melancholics tend to hold grudges because they are intense and deep. Phlegmatics sometimes avoid necessary confrontation because they want peace.

Some weaknesses are the result of our biochemistry. Certain groups have a higher incidence of alcoholism, for example. Other weaknesses can result from not enough discipline in our upbringing or, conversely, discipline that was too harsh. Violence begets more violence, as the saying goes. Sometimes we are not aware of a weakness until we undergo some kind of trial. A person might not realize he has an anger problem, for example, until he comes unglued at a stressful job. As with strengths, over time our weaknesses can become habits, or even compulsions, that rob us of peace and joy. If left unchecked, they can turn into vices that prevent us from choosing those things that are truly good for us.

Hopefully this information helps you to think a little more about your strengths and weaknesses. With it in mind, continue to the next question.

2. What are your strengths?

Rank the choices below from 1 to 8, with 1 being your greatest strength and 8 being the strength that applies to you the least.

- ____ Perseverance—I have stamina and can stay committed to a goal for a long time.
- ____ Boldness—I am willing to take risks to serve others.
- ____ Trustworthiness—I tell the truth and maintain the confidence of others.
- ____ Loyalty—My friends can rely on me.
- ____ Good Stewardship—I manage my time and resources wisely.
- ____ Self-Control—I can easily say no to bad things and yes to good things.
- ____ Discernment—I can easily discern the best option in a complex situation.
- ____ Initiative—I can take initiative and commit to a course of action without delay.

3. What are your weaknesses?

Rank the list below from 1 to 8, with 1 being your greatest weakness and 8 being the weakness that applies to you the least.

___ Inconstancy—I tend to lose focus and energy on projects and people.

___ Cowardice—I am often afraid of initiating something and fail to make decisions in a timely manner.

___ Untrustworthiness—I often lie or alter the truth to suit my own needs or ideas.

___ Envy—I tend to resent the possessions or successes of others rather than be happy for them.

___ Bad Stewardship—I tend to waste time and money on unimportant things.

___ Lack of Self-Control—I often struggle with strong impulses and saying no to harmful behaviors.

___ Busyness—I often fail to discern my true priorities and at times involve myself in unimportant activities.

___ Bossiness—I tend to think too highly of my own desires and opinions and to pressure others to do what I want.

Temperament Assessment

God made each one of us unique. We have a unique set of talents, skills, and attitudes. Some of these talents, skills, and attitudes are innate, meaning that they are just part of who we are, while others are learned and shaped by our experiences in life. The ones that are innate often correspond to our temperament. To find out which temperament you have, answer questions 4–7 while thinking about your natural inclinations and tendencies.

4. Which of these phrases would you use to describe yourself?

Rank them 1 to 4, with 1 being the phrase that describes you the most and 4 being the term that describes you the least.

___ Peace-Builder—I enjoy helping people reach a win-win.

___ Go-Getter—I tend to take charge in order to lead people to a goal.

___ People-Person—I am energized by meeting people and building relationships.

___ Deep-Thinker—I am motivated by ideas and big questions.

5. Which description below best matches your natural disposition?

Check one of the following:

___ I am focused on *peace*. I tend to be rational, orderly, and motivated by a sense of completion and harmony. I tend to approach things scientifically, but I am open to evaluating and seeing other perspectives. When encountering a problem or a task, I often ask myself what needs to be done to fix it. I tend to be the restrained one in group settings. I am not often upset, as long as everyone is being heard and invited to participate.

___ I am focused on *ideas*. I tend to be very deep and need time for reflection in order to consider ideas and their consequences. I am typically self-motivated, and what really matters to me is not being rewarded or praised but knowing that I have been true to the idea. Friends consider me naturally loyal, faithful, and stable. When encountering a problem or a task, I often ask myself what is the purpose and how will we evaluate the outcome. I tend to be deeper and quieter in group settings. I am not often upset as long as the purpose and the outcome of the task have been clearly identified.

___ I am focused on *action*. I tend to have a lot of energy and enthusiasm, and I am typically self-confident. Sometimes people see me as too intense. I enjoy competition. I am aware of the talents I have, and I can lead people to use their talents. When encountering a problem or a task, I ask myself what is the goal and how do we achieve it. I tend to take charge in group settings and am upset by lack of action.

___ I am focused on *people and relationships*. I tend to have a lot of compassion for others, and I love to be creative and spontaneous. Relationships and working with others motivate me. I am humorous and can easily befriend others. My circle of friends is relatively large, and I can bond with people I meet very quickly. When encountering a problem or a task, I ask myself who will be there and what will we do? I tend to talk a lot in group settings, and I am upset when not everyone is participating.

6. Considering the descriptions above, which statement below describes you best? Which one describes you least?

Rank them 1–4, with 1 being the statement that describes you best and 4 being the statement that describes you least.

___ I am generally focused on peace.
___ I am generally focused on people.
___ I am generally focused on action.
___ I am generally focused on ideas.

7. Which virtues (or good habits) do you need to work on the most?

Choose your top 5 and rank them 1–5, with 1 being the virtue you need to work on the most and 5 the virtue you need to work on the least.

___ Faith—I need to believe more fully in the truths God has revealed about Himself and His plan for me.
___ Hope—I need more confidence in God's goodness and readiness to help me.
___ Love—I need to grow in my ability to love God above all things and to love my neighbor as myself.
___ Prudence—I need to make wiser and healthier decisions.
___ Self-Control—I need to do a better job controlling strong impulses and avoiding harmful behaviors.
___ Justice—I need to be more attentive about giving others what they are due.
___ Courage—I need to respond more bravely to what each situation demands.
___ Humility—I need to be more accepting of the truth about myself. I need to be more honest about my strengths and weaknesses, while accepting that God made me His child and loves me.
___ Obedience—I need to do more quickly and with less complaining what I know is right and what honors my commitments and responsibilities.
___ Compassion—I need to share more gladly in the sufferings of others.

____ Generosity—I need to give more of myself in helping and serving others.

____ Honor—I need to recognize my own dignity and more readily act accordingly.

____ Greatheartedness—I need to trust more that when God asks me to do challenging things, He will give me what I need to do them.

____ Gratitude—I need to be more thankful for all the gifts and blessings God gives me every day.

____ Wonder—I need to grow in my awareness of all the beauty that surrounds me and in my ability to be filled with awe at the greatness of the Creator.

____ Cooperation—I need to be more cooperative when working toward a common goal with others.

What The Spiritual Audit Reveals about You

Your primary temperament

Check the statement that applies to you.

____ If your answers above focus on peace, then your temperament is *phlegmatic.*

____ If your answers above focus on action, then your temperament is *choleric.*

____ If your answers above focus on ideas, then your temperament is *melancholic.*

____ If your answers above focus on people and relationships, then your temperament is *sanguine.*

Your secondary temperament

Most people are a combination of two temperaments. Some people are strong in both, with one only slightly more dominant than the other, while others are strongly dominant in one temperament, with only traces of another temperament.

In your answer to question 6 (p. 52), which description did you rank as number 2? That is your secondary temperament. Write it here:

_____

Finding your temperament combination
Below is a list of all the possible temperament combinations: *choleric/ sanguine, choleric/melancholic, sanguine/choleric, sanguine/phlegmatic, phlegmatic/sanguine, phlegmatic/melancholic, melancholic/phlegmatic,* and *melancholic/choleric.* In each pair, the dominant temperament is mentioned first. Find the combination that matches your answers to questions 4–6 (pp. 50–52) and write it here:

_____

Now do the following:

1. Examine the strengths and weaknesses of your temperament combination below and compare them to what you indicated as your strengths and weaknesses in questions 2 and 3 (pp 49–50). If there is a particular strength you are really good at below, underline it. If there is a particular weakness or compulsion that you really struggle with, circle it.

2. Review the virtues in your temperament combination. Then look again at the virtues you identified in question 7 (pp 52–53). In the lines provided below your temperament combination, write the five virtues that you would like to develop, with 1 being the virtue you need to work on most. The next part of the book reviews each of the virtues in detail. The third part of the book will help you to create an action plan for growing in the virtues you need to work on the most.

3. Also examine the common vices that your temperament combination typically struggles with. Circle any vices that challenge you. Put a line through any vices that you have avoided or have made progress in overcoming. Ask God for the strength to continue overcoming them.

Choleric/Sanguine: The Pace-Setter
Strengths
  ◦ Boldness, Initiative
Weaknesses
  ◦ Busyness, Bossiness, Lack of Self-Control
Common Vices
  ◦ Pride, Rashness, Vanity, Lust, Envy
Virtues Needed
  ◦ Humility, Self-Control, Prudence (as in Deliberation)

1. _____

2. _____

3. _____

4. _____

5. _____

Choleric/Melancholic: The Problem-Solver

Strengths
   ◦ Perseverance, Loyalty, Initiative
Weaknesses
   ◦ Bossiness, Envy
Common Vices
   ◦ Pride (as well as Intellectual Pride), Anger, Cynicism
Virtues Needed
   ◦ Humility, Cooperation, Compassion, Gratitude

1. _____

2. _____

3. _____

4. _____

5. _____

Sanguine/Choleric: The Life-of-the-Party

Strengths
   ◦ Boldness, Initiative, Loyalty
Weaknesses
   ◦ Lack of Self-Control, Bad Stewardship, Busyness
Common Vices
   ◦ Rashness, Pride, Lust, Gluttony, Vanity
Virtues Needed
   ◦ Courage (as in Perseverance), Humility, Justice, Prudence

1. _____

2. _____

3. _____

4. _____

5. _____

Sanguine/Phlegmatic: The Diplomat

Strengths
  ○ Loyalty, Good Stewardship, Trustworthiness
Weaknesses
  ○ Lack of Self-Control, Cowardice, Inconstancy
Common Vices:
  ○ Lust, Rashness, Vanity, Intellectual Pride
Virtues Needed
  ○ Courage (as in Perseverance), Self-Control, Humility

1. _____

2. _____

3. _____

4. _____

5. _____

Phlegmatic/Sanguine: The Peacekeeper

Strengths
  ○ Trustworthiness, Good Stewardship, Discernment
Weaknesses
  ○ Cowardice
Common Vices
  ○ Cowardice, Laziness
Virtues Needed
  ○ Greatheartedness, Obedience, Courage

1. _____

2. _____

3. _____

4. _____

5. _____

Phlegmatic/Melancholic: The Planner

Strengths
 ◦ Loyalty, Trustworthiness, Good Stewardship, Self-Control, Discernment
Weaknesses
 ◦ Cowardice, Inconstancy
Common Vices
 ◦ Cynicism, Laziness, Cowardice
Virtues Needed
 ◦ Greatheartedness, Courage, Compassion

1. _____

2. _____

3. _____

4. _____

5. _____

Melancholic/Phlegmatic: The Scholar

Strengths
 ◦ Discernment, Self-Control, Loyalty
Weaknesses
 ◦ Cowardice
Common Vices
 ◦ Despair, Cynicism, Intellectual Pride, Cowardice
Virtues Needed
 ◦ Courage (as in Audacity), Prudence (as in Decision), Humility, Cooperation

1. _____

2. _____

3. _____

4. _____

5. _____

Melancholic/Choleric: The Goal-Setter

Strengths
  ◦ Perseverance, Loyalty
Weaknesses
  ◦ Bossiness
Common Vices
  ◦ Despair, Anger, Wrath, Intellectual Pride
Virtues Needed
  ◦ Courage (as in Audacity), Humility, Compassion, Obedience

1. _____

2. _____

3. _____

4. _____

5. _____

Part 2

The Habits That Bring Life

5

The Power of the Will

"Do not be conformed to this world but be transformed by the renewal of your mind, that you may prove what is the will of God, what is good and acceptable and perfect."

—Romans 12:2

In the previous chapters, we touched on the importance of the will. We spoke about why Christians and all people who want more freedom and less negativity ought to spend more time developing the habits that give life and subduing those habits that rob us of joy. The Spiritual Audit likely confirmed what you already knew about yourself, and hopefully it provides more clarity about your temperament. It also identifies which vices you need to tame and which virtues you need to strengthen.

Before focusing on the individual virtues and how to develop them into powerful and life-giving habits, it is necessary to give a more detailed account of the will. Perhaps Victor Hugo summed up the importance of the will best: "People do not lack strength; they lack will."[1] Each person can choose to have one of the following: a weak will, a strong will, or a good will. A weak will leads to being overpowered by bad habits, and a strong will that simply wants to gratify one's ego is the result of pride. A good will, on the other hand, seeks what is good, beautiful, and true—and not just for oneself but for everyone. A good will wants what God wants, and prays to the Father in the words of Jesus: "Not my will, but yours, be done" (Lk 22:42).

How do we know the will of God? As Saint Paul said: "Do not be conformed to this world, but be transformed by the renewal of your mind, that you may prove what is the will of God, what is good and acceptable and perfect" (Rom 12:2). This is the Christian message that we need to reclaim and live out in bold and adventurous ways if we are to become the men and women God intends us to be.

Be Perfect

Jesus culminates His central teaching in the first part of the Sermon on the Mount by saying, "You, therefore, must be perfect, as your heavenly Father is perfect" (Mt 5:48). He doesn't mean just be a generally good person—no, He means for us to become sons and daughters of God by forming and exercising our will in order to do God's will. This requires us to grow in self-control, for Saint Paul said, "This is the will of God ... that each one of you know how to control his own body in holiness and honor" (1 Thess 4:4). The apostles knew this would not be easy. That's why Peter reminded his flock to think about the suffering of Jesus: "Since therefore Christ suffered in the flesh, arm yourselves with the same thought ... so as to live for the rest of the time in the flesh no longer by human passions but by the will of God" (1 Pt 4:1–2). In other words, enduring hardship and trial, in union with the sufferings of Christ, is the way our will becomes perfected and more capable of saying yes to God without reserve.

Our will is vitally important; along with our intellect it is what makes us like our heavenly Father, who created us in His image and likeness. Since we can freely choose our actions, we are therefore capable of love or its opposite, sin. But God does not force us to love. As Catholic author Dr. John Wood has said, God "may be King, but he is not a dictator. We have free will, so we choose our freedom, and we choose our slavery. As long as we continue to choose pride, envy, greed, anger, sloth, gluttony, and lust, we will be slaves."[2]

Because of the Fall, we are born with a weakened will and a tendency to sin. Then our own sins and those of others wound our wills even more. We cannot heal our wounded condition without God's help, but God doesn't impose His help on us. As Saint Francis de Sales explained, God doesn't want merely our permission to help us, but our desire to be restored to a relationship with Him, "for permission is an action of the will which of itself is barren, sterile and fruitless, and is as it were a passive action, which acts not but only permits action; desire on the contrary is an active, fruitful, fertile action, which excites, invites and urges."[3] It's not enough to give God permission to work in our lives and then sit idly by. We must *desire* to receive God's love and to love Him in return—by our obedience. "For this is the love of God, that we keep his commandments" (1 Jn 5:3).

It is neither all God, nor all us. It is God and us. We must cooperate with God, because He gave us the gift of free will so that we could love like Him by loving Him and others. And why do we love God? "We love, because he first loved us" (1 Jn 4:19). God is the one who initiates this cycle of love, and we should take great comfort from that. This was the whole point of God's becoming man, to show His love for us by suffering death on a cross for our sakes. God wants to save you. He wants to redeem and restore you. He wants to help you become who you really are. He wants you to be happy with Him in this life and in the life to come. He asks only that we cooperate with Him, not with a will that is too weak to get up and follow Him or with a will that is too strong to let Him take the lead, but with a will that is eager to say yes.

The Weak Will

The weak will is not to be confused with a docile will. A docile will is obedient to the truth and the demands of authentic love, whereas the weak will is dominated by the appetite and often aligns itself with its immediate and often sinful desires. Weak-willed people are motivated by the lower levels of happiness. They can even become slaves to their appetites if they do not learn to conform their will to what is truly good. A weak-willed person is prone to abdicating responsibility and refusing to participate in the drama of becoming who He is called to be. It is important to know that a weak will can be found in both the reckless sinner and the overbearing religious zealot.

As Christians we are familiar with images of the repentant reckless sinner—the lost sheep who is found, the Prodigal Son who returns home, in other words the person who realizes that following his passions is not leading to real happiness, and turns around. In a way, this is the story of each of us to lesser or greater degrees. All of us have experienced flashes of understanding that a sinful behavior is not bringing the happiness we thought it would. That in fact it is causing us, and others too, misery. In those moments, we recognized that we are sinners who have offended God and others, and cannot save ourselves. We knew we needed God to forgive us and to help us begin anew.

Many of us are also familiar with the image of the fearful religious zealot, the pietistic hypocrite who lives in fear of failing. These are tough words, but this is how many non-believers characterize Christians. To never sin out of love is a beautiful thing indeed. To repent in sorrow of sin is also beautiful. But to doubt God's love and mercy, such that one is fearful to exercise his free will, is contrary to the Christian life. It is based on a faulty image of God. We need to understand God as a loving father who wants what is best for His child. He does not want His child to be good out of fear of punishment, but rather out of loving obedience and relationship. Saint Francis de Sales wrote, "We cannot help conforming ourselves to what we love.... [If a man has] love there is no need to press him by the rigour of the law, love being the most pressing teacher and solicitor, to urge the heart which it possesses to obey the will and the intention of the beloved."[4]

It is important here to note that certain temperaments tend to have weaker wills. Sanguines and phlegmatics are more ephemeral and can struggle to form and to exercise their wills. If your temperament is sanguine/phlegmatic or phlegmatic/sanguine, pay special attention. If you are a mix of choleric and sanguine or melancholic and phlegmatic, this may be less of an issue.

Sanguines have lots of energy for people and relationships and tend toward being more motivated by their senses. This does not mean that they struggle with sin any more or any less than the other temperaments. However, their wills can easily be divided, and whatever thing is more pressing, more urgent, and more attuned to relationships and the senses will get most attention. They tend to abdicate their will to the will of others or to the particular needs of a situation. The sanguine always needs to focus on the virtue of temperance, or self-control (see chapter 10 on the virtue of temperance).

Phlegmatics have lots of energy for building consensus and seeking peace. They strive to maintain harmony in their relationships. However, easily overcome by their revulsion to conflict, they tend to avoid sometimes necessary confrontations. Phlegmatics tend to abdicate their will for the good of the group and are less likely to speak up if others in the group agree with each other. The phlegmatic always needs to grow in the virtue of courage and to learn to assert his will in constructive ways (see chapter 11 on the virtue of courage).

The Strong Will

The strong will, as we are using the term here, is not to be confused with the will that seeks greatness. The will that seeks greatness courageously discerns and chooses the good and directs the appetite toward it. The strong will, on the other hand, is dominated by taking action and often asserts itself independently of the intellect or the consideration of anyone else. If the weak will is often too inconsistent and flighty, then the strong will is often too stubborn and self-righteous. Strong-willed people are motivated by their ego and their belief that their way is the right way and the only way. If they do not learn to submit to the will of others, they can become selfish and domineering, while assuming that they are helping others when they are really only seeking to help themselves. The strong-willed person tends to dominate others. He also is reluctant to let others participate in his becoming the person he is called to be. It is important to know that a strong will can be found in both the stoic loner and the self-righteous leader.

The stoic loner is the self-assured thinker who cannot be convinced of anything that he has not concluded on his own. We are familiar with the caricature of the know-it-all who does not consider the ideas of those with opposing views. In fact, such a person often shows contempt toward those who disagree with him.

The self-righteous leader is the person of action whose will dominates and even destroys the will of others. He not only knows the solution; he knows what he must do and cannot be convinced otherwise. People who disagree or suggest other ways to address the problem are often seen as obstacles rather than allies. This stubbornness often reveals itself as an "I know best, and you are either with me or against me" attitude. Such a person often cannot admit failure without blaming someone else. In extreme cases, this type of person asserts his will by trying to control the will of others, either through manipulation or force. He often assumes that he has things figured out and is not easily humbled. In the Western world, the strong-willed person is sometimes seen as the natural leader, as he takes charge of situations and gets things done. However, a strong will does not on its own qualify a person to lead, and it does not ensure that a person will lead others to a good place.

Those with strong wills have a difficult time surrendering and submitting to God. One reason is that they have a hard time admitting that they have been wrong or that they need guidance from outside themselves. In his excellent book *The Purpose Driven Life*, Pastor Rick Warren explained that in our competitive society we do not hear much about surrendering. "If winning is everything, surrendering is unthinkable. We would rather talk about winning, succeeding, overcoming, and conquering than yielding, submitting, obeying, and surrendering. But surrendering to God is the heart of worship. It is the natural response to God's amazing love and mercy. We give ourselves to Him, not out of fear or duty, but in love, because 'He first loved us.' "[5]

It is important here to note that certain temperaments tend to have stronger wills. Cholerics and melancholics are more stable and constant and need to be challenged to align their wills with their intellects in order to serve and direct their appetites. If your temperament is choleric/melancholic or melancholic/choleric, pay special attention. If you are a mix of choleric and sanguine or melancholic and phlegmatic, this may be less of an issue for you.

Cholerics have lots of energy for action and sustained activity for a long time. They are motivated by getting things done. They often have a strong will that needs to be well-formed and directed to seek the help of others. The choleric is too easily convinced that his motives, methods, and ends are the right ones, therefore he must learn to ask himself: "Just because I can do this, should I do this?" The choleric needs to grow in the virtue of prudence (see chapter 8). He needs to think before he acts and to reflect on his motives, methods, and ends. He must learn to seek the counsel of others to help with discerning and acting accordingly.

The melancholic is naturally reflective and is motivated by ideas. Much of his emotion and insight comes from deep and sustained internal reflection and analysis. He is often slow to respond, but has great depth, passion, and richness in his response. The melancholic's will is formed in his own mind; once set on an idea, a melancholic is unlikely to change course. Since melancholics are naturally deep and thoughtful, any attempt to change their mind is often met with resistance. While the choleric's will is forceful, the melancholic's will is often unchangeable. The melancholic temperament needs to grow in the virtue of confidence, as in greateartedness or magnanimity (see chapter 16 on this virtue). He also needs greater trust in his ability to contribute to the common good, not just in his ideas but in his actions as well.

The weak and strong wills are both insufficient to guide the human heart to happiness. The weak will can be overcome by its appetite, and the strong will often cannot be directed by its intellect. The goal for each person, and especially for those who call themselves Christian, is to have a *good will*. People with a good will respond well and act in accordance with the truth of how God has made them (their temperament) and who God has called them to be (their character).

The Good Will

As we have said, the will moves our heart and mind toward something we desire and moves our heart and mind away from something we do not desire. Put simply, our will is the part of us that chooses. When we make a choice, we are exercising our will. As discussed in previous chapters, in addition to our will we also have natural inclinations and appetites, and we also have our reason and intellect. The good will aligns with the intellect to direct the appetite toward what is good, beautiful, and true. Put another way, the good will is not divided or at war with the appetite or intellect.

Consider the decision-making process of a person with a good will. The person will discern by consulting the intellect, by asking questions such as "Is this the right thing to do?", "Do I need this?", "Is this consistent with who I am?", "Does doing this make me more of who I am called to be?", "Is this what Jesus would want?" The person will also consider the appetite. "Do I want this?", "Is now the right time?", "Is there something I want more?" "Is there something I need that is more important?" The person with a weak will may avoid such questions in the first place. The strong-willed person will simply answer yes to all the questions without thinking it through, or, despite answering no, do it anyway.

The person with a good will delights in asking such questions. And here is the most important part, he does what he discerns and decides to do. It is worth noting here that the intellect plays a really important role in all of this. In order to help direct the will, we must properly reason, and we must know ourselves and the truths of the natural world. The will and the intellect must learn to work together, however, because the intellect cannot on its own move the will.

Saint John Henry Newman reminds us, in his classic text *Grammar of Assent*, that knowing something does not guarantee we will act on it. We can know something and believe it to be true, but that knowledge on its own does not have a moral force. Many of us know that that some of our habits are bad, sinful, and that they kill our joy and steal our peace, but we do them anyway. The moral force for action comes from our will, which chooses to accept and to live in accordance with correct knowledge or to reject it so as to choose that which we know is wrong. The tendency of the will to rebel against reason and to choose instead to fulfill a disordered desire is called *concupiscence*. And we all have it, thanks to original sin.

When Jesus encounters Nathaniel (also called Bartholomew) under the fig tree in the Gospel of John, He says that there is "no guile" within him (1:47). In other words, Nathaniel is not duplicitous, crafty, or deceitful. He talks and acts in ways that are consistent with his mind and heart. Jesus sees the good will in Nathaniel and knows that the next three years of their time together will make Nathaniel into not only a good-willed person, but a great-willed person. Judas, on the other hand, is duplicitous and eventually treacherous. Iconographers depicting the Last Supper illustrate this by showing only the right side of his face, to say that he is hiding the sinister side from us. Judas is divided in his will.

You may be surprised to learn that if your will is too weak, the goal of *WillPower Advantage* is *not* to make it stronger. If your will is too strong, the goal is *not* to make it weaker. Rather, *the goal is to make our will good, better, and more capable of partnering with our intellect to choose the good, which brings us life and joy, and to reject the bad, which steals our peace and joy and ultimately brings death.*

The will aligned with the intellect, directing our appetites toward what is good, beautiful, and true is the vision that God has for each one of us. He wants us to form our will to be good, so that we can choose Him and His plan for our happiness, and thus reject the temptations that would lead us astray. He wants us to be men and women after His own heart. He longs for our hearts to be conformed to His.

This is the definition of a saint: someone whose will is so aligned with God's will that he begins to live for heaven while still here on earth. If you know the saints, you know that they are all unique. God, through His grace, helps them to overcome their sins, but they do not overcome their nature. Rather, grace perfects their nature. Their temperament, their experiences, their foibles, their quirks aren't destroyed by aligning their will with God's will for them, rather they are redeemed and made free to contribute to making them who they are called to be. Perhaps this is what Saint Paul had in mind when he wrote, "We know that in everything God works for good with those who love him, who are called according to his purpose" (Rom 8:28). Even our weakness God uses to form us and make us strong. The Lord told Saint Paul, "My grace is sufficient for you, for my power is made perfect in weakness." Thus, Paul concluded, "I will all the more gladly boast of my weaknesses, that the power of Christ may rest upon me" (2 Cor 12:9).

All the saints testify to this truth. The early Church Fathers called Our Blessed Mother Mary the first saint. She has been invoked for millennia as the Queen of the Saints. She is an example par excellence of a good will! Mary was completely docile to the Holy Spirit when she answered the angel, "Behold, I am the handmaid of the Lord; let it be to me according to your word" (Lk 1:38). Her entire life was a constant "let it be" (in Latin, *fiat*), a continuous yes to the Lord. It was not a weak or naïve yes, nor was it an arrogant or strong yes. It was an abiding yes, trusting in God and desiring His will for her life.

The goal of *The WillPower Advantage* is to help Christians have *good wills*, and to grow in the virtues needed to become the men and women that their families, churches, and communities so desperately need. It is about helping Christians be the Christian heroes that this world needs. So, how do we conform our wills to God's? How do we change our weak or strong will into a good will? We grow in virtue.

The first part of this book was focused on knowing the battle and knowing yourself. Armed with this knowledge let us move into the second part and dive deep into developing the habits that give life, bring peace, and yield joy.

6

The Habits That Bring Life

"I have set before you life and death, blessing and curse;
therefore choose life, that you and your descendants may live."

—Deuteronomy 30:19

Aristotle famously said that "we are what we repeatedly do." Now,
Aristotle was a smart guy, and listening to him and the other ancient
Greeks who helped build Western civilization is not a bad idea.
However, let us carefully examine this statement. It is true that the
things we do over and over begin to become habits and to define part
of who we are. In the words of the always quotable Vince Lombardi,
"Winning is a habit. Unfortunately, so is losing."[1] Our occupations
and our talents are cultivated by consistent practice, or they are not
grown due to our neglect. We become a musician, not by just claiming the title, but by repeatedly playing and perfecting an instrument.
It is much the same way for a baker, an artist, and even for mothers
and fathers. We become good at things by doing them repeatedly,
sometimes with disciplined practice, until we begin to perfect our
skills. We agree with Aristotle that you become a good person by
doing the things that make a person good. Jesus and the saints would
likely add that you become a happy and holy person by doing things
that make a person happy and holy.

But there is more to the story. First, as Christians we believe that
our sinful habits do not ultimately define us, although these bad habits can hinder us from becoming who we are made to be. When Pope
Saint John Paul II gathered with over one million youth in Toronto,
he reminded us, "*We are not the sum of our weaknesses and failures;
we are the sum of the Father's love for us and our real capacity to*

become the image of His Son."² This is good news, in fact it is great news! But remembering who we are and behaving like a beloved son or daughter is not always easy. It takes work, much practice, picking up ourselves after failures, dusting off our souls in the Sacrament of Reconciliation, and building virtues as if they were spiritual muscles! As Saint James explained, we must become who we are with faith accompanied by works (see Jas 2:14).

Second, we are called to be *more than good*. As beloved sons and daughters of the Father, we are called to be people of the beatitudes. Beatitudes are the dispositions or the reasons we act in certain ways, which Jesus articulated in His Sermon on the Mount. They describe not only the virtuous person, but the person who lives in a way that points toward God's kingdom in heaven. This is why, for the Christian, the virtues do not stop at just being a good person. When combined with God's grace, the virtues also dispose us toward being in deep, personal, and *personalized* relationship with God—meaning a son or a daughter alive in His kingdom. The virtues and the beatitudes are intimately connected, a theme that will be further developed in the following chapters. For example, when Jesus says, "Blessed are the meek, for they shall inherit the earth" (Mt 5:5), He is saying that only those with the virtues of humility and magnanimity—i.e., the meek—can receive and interact with the world in the way God had intended before the Fall. God wants us to develop and to grow in virtue so that we have more happiness and peace in our lives, and so that we are more prepared to participate in His kingdom, both on earth and ultimately in heaven.

Becoming Virtuous

The goal of *The WillPower Advantage* is to help people become virtuous—cooperating with God's grace to cultivate the habits that bring life, holiness, and peace to them and those around them. These habits, or virtues, are the keys to life, and they prepare the Christian to start living in and enjoying God's kingdom here on earth, while waiting to live it fully with Him and all the saints and the angels in heaven. This cannot be overstated: virtues really are crucial. It is really very simple. A virtue is a habit of choosing the good, and the more good choices we make, the happier and more fulfilled we are, the more peace we have, and the more open we become to doing God's work in building His kingdom.

Just because this concept is simple, doesn't mean it is easy! Far from it. Acquiring virtues takes discipline, training, and awareness of the spiritual opposition you will face whenever you try to grow into a better person. Choosing not to eat all the cheesecake is not easy for the person who really, really likes cheesecake, and choosing not to get angry in traffic is not easy for the person who is prone to losing his temper. Believe us, we know! Developing the virtues is like working out spiritual muscles. The more you use and develop them, the stronger they become, and the easier it is to choose the good over the bad. As you develop a good habit, it helps you to make the better choice, time and time again. And it retrains your brain, your heart, and your will.

There is no such thing as an accidental virtue. You do not just develop the virtue of courage by accidently doing something brave, any more than you accidently become a musician by dropping a guitar and making a sound. Virtue, by definition, is intentional. A virtuous act is chosen by you. To be a virtuous act it must have a good end in mind and good means to that end. In other words, to grow in virtue, you must desire the good, choose the good, and do the good. Over time, a virtue can become almost second nature, as with any habit, but it sure doesn't begin that way!

The Virtues

Some virtues are given to us by God. They are free gifts that we must not only accept but also put to use. Traditionally we call these the *supernatural virtues*. They are faith, hope, and love.

- *Faith* is believing that what God has revealed is true, not because it seems true but because it has come from God.
- *Hope* is trusting that God will provide everything necessary to reach ultimate happiness with Him in heaven.
- *Love* is loving God above all things for His own sake and loving others.

"So faith, hope, love abide, these three," wrote Saint Paul, "but the greatest of these is love" (1 Cor 13:13). Saint Peter said, "Above all hold unfailing your love for one another, since love covers a multitude of sins" (1 Pt 4:8). In the end, all that will matter will be how well we obeyed the two greatest commandments—to love God and to love neighbor (Mt 22:36–40). "At the evening of life," wrote Saint John of the Cross, "we shall be judged on our love."[3]

We receive the supernatural virtues of faith, hope, and love at our Baptism, and they are developed in our lives by our accepting them more completely over time. God infuses them into our very hearts, and we can either accept and use them, or reject them and leave them unused, like an opened gift that sits on the closet shelf and gets dusty.

The other virtues, sometimes called the *moral or human virtues*, are not like the supernatural virtues, as they are developed only through purposeful choice and action on our part. "The moral virtues are acquired by human effort. They are the fruit and seed of morally good acts; they dispose all the powers of the human being for communion with divine love."[4] Traditionally there are four central or *cardinal* (Latin for "hinge") virtues, on which the other virtues depend. They are prudence, temperance, justice, and fortitude.

- *Prudence* is making wise and healthy decisions.
- *Temperance*, or self-control, is choosing good things, in the right amount, and rejecting bad things.
- *Justice* is giving others what they are due.
- *Fortitude*, or courage, is bravely responding to what each situation demands.

The three supernatural virtues and the four cardinal virtues make up the list of seven virtues that have traditionally been taught by the Church.

There are many different lists of virtues. There are the classical seven, the forty named by various educational authors, those prized by ancient Rome, and those valued today. Whatever the list, virtue is always connected to what we *will* (our choice) and what we do (our action). As taught by Aristotle, virtue is the mean (i.e., the middle) between the extremes of defect (too little) and excess (too much). Thus to us, seven virtues seem too few and forty too many. So we will focus on thirteen virtues that we believe are the essential *core virtues* for human flourishing and Christian discipleship. These are also the most crucial for the Christian who is seeking to become the man or the woman that God has made each one of us to be. We'll briefly review them here, and we will go into greater depth in the following chapters.

Each chapter will provide a definition of the virtue, its relationship to the beatitudes, and some insight into that particular virtue. It will relate the virtue to your temperament, review the corresponding vice, and offer some practical advice on how to grow in that virtue. In order to decide which chapters to read first, we recommend that you look back at your Spiritual Audit and start with the virtues that you need to develop most.

Here is *The WillPower Advantage* list of the thirteen core virtues:

- Compassion—sharing in the sufferings and the joys of others
- Prudence—making wise and healthy decisions
- Justice—giving others what they are due
- Self-Control—behaving with moderation
- Courage—bravely responding to what each situation demands
- Humility—living in the truth about your strengths and weaknesses
- Obedience—doing what you know is right and what you ought to do
- Generosity—giving abundantly in the service of others
- Honor—recognizing your own dignity and acting accordingly
- Greatheartedness—trusting that you have been called to do great things and daring to do them with confidence
- Gratitude—giving thanks for all that you have
- Wonder—being filled with awe at the beauty and the complexity of creation
- Cooperation—working willingly toward a common goal with others

7

Compassion

"Rejoice with those who rejoice, weep with those who
weep."

—Romans 12:15

The virtue of compassion means having empathy for others and
being willing to share both their joys and suffering. *Compassion* literally means "to suffer with"; it involves having a deep feeling for
the misery of another person and the desire to relieve it. Sometimes
we associate compassion with the emotion of pity. However, compassion is never just emotion, as it demands putting love into action.
As the Nobel Laureate and Anglican Archbishop Desmond Tutu so
beautifully explained, "Compassion is not just feeling with someone,
but seeking to change the situation. Frequently people think compassion and love are merely sentimental. No! They are very demanding.
If you are going to be compassionate, be prepared for action!"[1]
It is hard to imagine, but many people in the ancient world thought
compassion was a weakness. Some Greek philosophers saw compassion as a vice because it was not logical to show concern for those
who didn't deserve it or couldn't repay you. There is one ancient
people, however, who stand out for their esteem for the virtue of
compassion—the Jews. The Old Testament is filled with praise and
guidance for being compassionate. After God freed the Israelites from
slavery in Egypt, He commanded them to be kind to strangers, since
they knew what it is like to be a stranger in a strange land (cf. Deut
10:19). There is constant exhortation to be compassionate to others,
because God has been compassionate to us. "The LORD is good to all;
and his compassion is over all that he has made" (Ps 145:9).

Jesus, Our Model

Jesus modeled compassion as a virtue, revealing more completely the heart of God. The Gospels say explicitly that Jesus had compassion—for the widow who lost her son (Lk 7:13), for example, and for the crowds who had been following Him and who were hungry (Mk 6: 34; 8:2). One story from the Gospels is exceptional in its personal details about Jesus—the death of Lazarus. When Jesus saw Mary, the sister of Lazarus, weeping, He was "deeply moved in spirit and troubled", and "Jesus wept" (Jn 11:33, 35). It is compassion, empathy for others, that moved Jesus to action, that compelled Him to heal the sick, feed the hungry, teach the people, forgive the sinner, and even raise the dead. The entire mission of Jesus, to bear all of our suffering with us and for us, proves that compassion is at the very heart of our Father, God.

The truly amazing thing about the compassion of God is that He bestows it on not only His friends but also His enemies. The truth is, when Jesus died for us, we were God's enemies. "God shows his love for us in that while we were yet sinners Christ died for us" (Rom 5:8). Jesus commanded us to be as generous with our compassion as God: "You have heard that it was said, 'You shall love your neighbor and hate your enemy.' But I say to you, Love your enemies and pray for those who persecute you, so that you may be sons of your Father who is in heaven; for he makes his sun rise on the evil and on the good, and sends rain on the just and on the unjust. For if you love those who love you, what reward have you?" (Mt 5:43–46).

The virtue of compassion is admired, but not often practiced in the radical way God desires. We judge, point fingers, assume the worst, and join others in condemnation more easily than we forgive, assume the best, give the benefit of the doubt, or defend those being unjustly criticized. On social media people often belittle, bully, slander, or otherwise behave in ways that can cause serious injury. Meanwhile, there is a good deal of virtue signaling going on, as if a person's opinions, rather than his concrete actions, prove that one has compassion. Imagine what it would look like if we took seriously Jesus' exhortation and put it into practice. To help us do that, let's look at two of His parables.

Two Parables

Of all the parables of Jesus, the two most well-known are the Prodigal Son and the Good Samaritan, and both of them contain the word *compassion*. One parable shows us the compassion that God has for us; the other shows us the compassion we ought to have for one another.

The Prodigal Son

In one of the most beautiful stories in all of Scripture, Jesus revealed the true love and compassion of our heavenly Father. The Parable of the Prodigal Son (Lk 15:11–32) begins with a young man asking his father for his inheritance and leaving home. After spending all of his money on "loose living" (v. 13), he ends up destitute and tending swine as a hired laborer. Humbled and famished, he decides to return to his father, confess his sin, and ask to be treated as a servant.

Jesus said that while the young man "was yet at a distance, his father saw him and had compassion, and ran and embraced him and kissed him" (v. 20). The father had every right to disown this son, who had forgotten who he was and squandered his inheritance, but instead the father rejoiced over the young man's return. He clothed him in his best robe, put a ring on his finger and sandals on his feet, and called for a feast. Oh, the compassion of the Father! His first instinct was not to punish his son but to restore him fully. His first move was not to point out what the son had done wrong, but to celebrate that he had done something right by returning. The father in the parable is an image of our Father in heaven, who is not angry when we sin, but sad that we have forgotten who we are and what He created us to be. He is full of compassion and waiting for us to turn around and come back to Him.

The Good Samaritan

The Gospel of Luke records that when Jesus explained that the greatest commandments are to love God and to love neighbor, one of the scribes asked Him, "And who is my neighbor?" Jesus responded with the Parable of the Good Samaritan:

> A man was going down from Jerusalem to Jericho, and he fell among robbers, who stripped him and beat him, and departed, leaving

him half dead. Now by chance a priest was going down that road; and when he saw him he passed by on the other side. So likewise a Levite, when he came to the place and saw him, passed by on the other side. But a Samaritan, as he journeyed, came to where he was; and when he saw him, he had compassion. (10:30–33)

The priest and the Levite were following their duty not to break the Jewish purity laws; however, they failed to follow the higher duty that we have to care for one another. The Jews had disdain for Samaritans because they did not follow the laws of Moses, so Jesus chose a Samaritan to show that compassion is the true meaning of the law. The Samaritan went to the beaten man and "bound up his wounds, pouring on oil and wine; then he set him on his own beast and brought him to an inn, and took care of him. And the next day he took out two denarii and gave them to the innkeeper, saying, 'Take care of him; and whatever more you spend, I will repay you when I come back'" (34–35).

After telling this story, Jesus asked, "Which of these three, do you think, proved neighbor to the man who fell among the robbers?" (34:36). Consider the following questions for a moment and allow the Holy Spirit to speak to your heart: Who is your neighbor? To whom are you called to show compassion? The scribe in the story answered, "The one who showed mercy on him." And Jesus said to him, "Go and do likewise" (v. 37). In the original Greek, the statement is even stronger. Jesus literally told the scribe and all those listening, "Go now and do the same thing!" If we are to have compassion for the stranger we do not know and who can't repay us, how much more are we to have compassion for our family, friends, and colleagues, as well as people in our churches, schools, offices, and even on the evening commute home.

Compassion is the virtue of heroes, of loving parents, and of good Samaritans who serve others without counting the cost or seeking a reward. Compassion is love in action, or if you prefer "love that has legs". It is one of the most sublime and heavenly virtues because it reflects the heart of God. Compassion makes the supernatural virtue of love visible in a broken and wounded world starving for love, hungering for authentic Christ-like heroes, which we are called to be!

Christ calls us to continue His work on earth by serving others with compassionate hearts. After He washed the apostles' feet, He said, "For I have given you an example, that you also should do as I have done to you" (Jn 13:15). The saints who have gone before us took seriously this mandate to serve others with compassion, and many people of faith continue to serve in creative and remarkable ways—in hospitals that care for the sick, soup kitchens that feed the poor, houses of hospitality that welcome the destitute, and so on. Our compassion for the wounds of others is a response to the compassion that God has shown us. It is a response to His call to love Him and to love one another as ourselves.

Other Examples of Compassion

Some of the most amazing stories are about people who are filled with the virtue of compassion, people who go beyond just feelings and take concrete steps to put their love into action. For nearly one hundred years *Reader's Digest* has included little stories about the kindness of strangers. While everyone is capable of being compassionate, as with any other virtue, compassion must be practiced in order to grow strong in us. Very often the compassionate people in these stories were not only in the right place at the right time (perhaps orchestrated by God), but practiced in the virtue of compassion and therefore ready to help when the need arose.

In one story, a woman driving home in a blizzard noticed a car trailing her closely. Suddenly her tire blew, and as she pulled over, so did the car that was following her. A man jumped out and without hesitation changed her tire. "I was going to get off two miles back," he said, "but I didn't think that tire looked good."[2] Simple stories of compassion like this one fill us with joy and speak to the goodness of men and women, who are created in God's own likeness. It is the scars and the wounds of sin in the world that tarnish our true identity.

What is often very telling in stories like this is that the people who do acts of service refuse any reward or adulation! They say things like "I was happy to help" or "I was lucky to be there" or my favorite "I know that someone would have done the same for me." In 2019 Danny Trejo, an actor who plays some of Hollywood's best-known villains, saved a baby that was trapped in a rolled-over car. When

asked by reporters for a comment, he said simply, "Everything good
that has happened to me has happened as a direct result of helping someone else. Everything."[3] As Scripture teaches: "It is more
blessed to give than to receive" (Acts 20:35). Compassion is the virtue of heroes, and every Christian should be filled and guided by it.
Our world needs more Christian heroes, and God has equipped and
anointed you to be one.

Since compassion is love in action, it can take many forms. It can
mean being patient with a difficult person as it did for the French
saint Thérèse of Lisieux. From the time she was a young girl, Thérèse
had a deep desire to serve God in dramatic ways. She wanted to be
a missionary in far-off lands, but due to poor health, she stayed close
to home in a small Carmelite monastery in France. She lived a quiet
life of compassionate and simple daily tasks, learning to serve God
by serving others, especially a cranky older sister in the Carmel. Her
"Little Way" was to do small things with great love. She wrote, "You
know well that Our Lord does not look so much at the greatness of
our actions, nor even at their difficulty, but at the love with which
we do them."[4] She modeled the axiom attributed to her, "At every
moment, do what love requires."

A more recent example of compassion is Saint Katharine Drexel
(1858–1955), the daughter of an affluent Philadelphia banker. She
learned from her generous parents how to share herself with others,
particularly the poor, and as a young adult she discerned a vocation
to religious life. At first she wanted to be a contemplative nun, but
the priest who was her spiritual director, who had become the first
bishop of Omaha, urged her to found a religious order to serve Blacks
and Native Americans. Katharine doubted her ability to do this, but
Bishop James O'Connor wrote her, "Even as a foundress, you will
have your faults, but God not you will do the work. He often makes
use of very weak instruments. The question is not will you be all you
should be, but does God will you to be his instrument."[5] Katharine
made a retreat to discern God's will, and at the end of it she committed herself to found the order the bishop had requested. On March 19,
1889, she wrote, "As long as I look on self, I cannot. Our Lord gives
and will give me the grace always to look at Him." Thus, Katharine
began the Sisters of the Blessed Sacrament. Under her leadership and
with funds from her large inheritance, the community founded 145

missions, fifty schools for African Americans, and twelve schools for Native Americans.

Katharine's compassion for the poor was guided by a deep sense of justice and a profound respect for the people she served. At a time when schools welcoming the children of Blacks and Native Americans were few, she committed herself to the principle that every child, regardless of skin color, wealth, or status, deserved an education. Her compassionate response to poverty and injustice, and her trust in God, continues to inspire us all.

A compassionate person knows the value of each person and wants what is truly good for each person. He sees everyone as a member of the one human family, with the same basic needs and desires as everyone else. Compassionate people think that we all have a responsibility toward each other, and they are willing to make sacrifices for others. They are not pushovers or sentimentalists; they are lovers of mankind who serve others with prudence and justice.

A Corresponding Beatitude

The beatitude that corresponds with the virtue of compassion is "Blessed are those who mourn, for they shall be comforted" (Mt 5:4). Mourning is not fun; it is difficult. Mourning is not something you choose to do but something that you experience after some great loss like the death of loved one. When someone mourns, he experiences intense feelings of sadness or emptiness.

To mourn well is not to suppress those sorrowful feelings, but to direct them toward something meaningful. In the case of the loss of a loved one, mourning leads to anguish and tears, but also to gratitude for the one who has died and for the gift of life itself, which is often taken for granted until one faces the reality of death. Mourning can lead to the realization that death is the result of sin having entered the world, and so the thing mourned is not only the loss but also the reality of sin. And that's why mourning in faith is a blessing (which is what the word *beatitude* means), because it leads to the comfort that comes from turning to God, who is compassionate, "merciful and gracious, slow to anger and abounding in mercy and faithfulness" (Ps 86:15).

Compassionate people are often those who have themselves suf-fered losses. Archbishop Fulton Sheen, who hosted a very popular television show in the 1950s, once explained that "it will invariably be found true that those who have suffered and who are saintly are always the most merciful to others."[6] Compassionate people react to the injustices and challenges others face with empathy (placing themselves in their shoes because they know well what being in those shoes feels like) and sympathy (accompanying them in their sadness or joy). When Jesus says blessed are those who mourn, he means all those who do not run away from the pain or discomfort caused by the brokenness of this world, but rather seek to heal, to redeem, and to restore the world to the way God intended His creation to be.

Compassion and the Temperaments

Your temperament is a gift from God, and as with any good gift, you must know what it is for and understand it well. While our temperaments are innate and natural, they are perfected by virtue. Compassion makes each of our temperaments more life-giving and beautiful. But for that to happen, you need to be aware of how your temperament impacts the way you grow in the virtue of compassion.

Choleric

People with a choleric temperament are motivated by action. They are doers and love to respond to a challenge. Because they are action-oriented, they sometimes fail to serve others with compassion. They may prioritize the task, the project, or the goal above the needs of individuals. They can be overly harsh and judgmental, especially toward people who do not have their same level of energy or will-ingness to endure hard work. Cholerics are protective of things they have invested in and worked on, so being compassionate toward family and friends may come easier. They need to work on applying their empathy, sympathy, and compassion to people outside their immediate circle. They need to develop the virtue of compassion to counteract the tendency to use people as means to their ends. A compassionate choleric is an incredible force to be reckoned with and can do great things in service of others.

Sanguine

People with the sanguine temperament love people and are motivated by relationships. Because they are more socially engaged, compassion and considering the needs of others come more naturally. They want to fix problems for those who are suffering and can have real empathy for the poor and needy. However, often compassion requires patience, and the sanguine temperament tends toward being quick and shallow. Sanguines need to develop the virtue of compassion in order to be patient and to bear the burdens of others. They are also easily offended and sensitive to not being appreciated. But compassion cannot be motivated by self-gain or self-satisfaction, and sanguines need to be willing to sacrifice for the sake of others and to forgive often in order to be compassionate.

Phlegmatic

People with the phlegmatic temperament are motivated by peace. They have a keen sense of justice and are drawn toward healing and restoring any brokenness they encounter. But this does not necessarily mean that they are naturally compassionate. Phlegmatics can sometimes be analytical and cold, and they need to temper their logic with compassion. They need to practice the virtue of compassion by seeing not just the problem to be solved, but the human being who is suffering and is in need. They need to allow their heart to be moved along with their head and ask themselves how to be most compassionate when serving others. The compassionate phlegmatic can do much to advance peace and justice for all mankind.

Melancholic

People with the melancholic temperament are motivated by ideas. They tend to be deep and have rich interior lives. They also tend to be direct and matter-of-fact. While they are in touch with their own emotions and feel deeply, they are often not intuitive about people they do not know well. They may come off as harsh, uncaring, and not compassionate when challenged with a particular individual in need. However, they are deeply justice-oriented, and the ideas of oppression, poverty, and suffering stir their hearts. The melancholic needs to cultivate the virtue of compassion by valuing equality, dignity, and love in their interpersonal relationships. Rather than seeing a person in need as a problem to solved, they must be willing to compassionately encounter and serve those in need. Compassionate melancholics can think deeply about human challenges, and they are capable of executing incredible ideas that restore justice, advance dignity, and promote love.

Associated Virtues

The virtue of compassion is assisted and practiced more readily when accompanied by these other virtues.

- *Kindness* is treating others as you want to be treated.
- *Sympathy* is acknowledging and trying to understand someone's pain or struggle.

Associated Vices

A lack of compassion can manifest itself in many ways, and we must be careful of these vices if we are to cultivate compassion.

- Anger—being overly displeased with a person or a situation. *Steals the joy of being in control of your emotions.*
- Wrath—desiring vengeance. *Steals the joy of showing mercy.*
- Apathy—not caring about the well-being of other people. *Steals the joy of loving others and serving their needs.*
- Envy—resenting the possessions or the successes of others. *Steals the joy of being happy for others.*

Practical Ways to Grow

That's the textbook stuff but let us talk for a moment about real compassion in action, and what it takes to develop this virtue at work, at home, and in life. To have compassion, a person needs four things:

1. Recognition of each person's innate dignity and worth
2. Willingness to let one's heart be moved to action
3. Willingness to sacrifice for the good of the other
4. Willingness to discern how one is called to respond compassionately in each situation

Unfortunately, many people often find Christians to be more judgmental than compassionate. God is full of compassion, so we should be as well. We are called to love others, even as we are called to hate sin. This is not a double standard or cop out. We can have compassion for the sinful, because we too are sinful and know that sin does not define us or them. The truth is that compassionate people are trusted and listened to, much more readily than the street preacher yelling that everyone, except him of course, is "going to hell". When Jesus walked the earth, He never stopped condemning sin, but He also never stopped loving and having compassion for the sinner. The adage, attributed to Theodore Roosevelt, "no one cares how much you know, until they know how much you care" rings true here. We must lead with compassion because we follow the Lord of compassion.

Jesus came "not to condemn the world, but that the world might be saved through him" (Jn 3:17). The world needs to see more Christians, not with a hand raised to condemn or strike, but a hand reaching out to help lift up and heal. When you and I reflect the compassion and mercy of Jesus, wounded hearts are healed, and the world begins to look a little less broken, and more like the Kingdom God has destined us to live in. Burt Bacharach was right: "What the world needs now is love, sweet love, no not just for some, but for everyone."[7] To put love into action we need the virtue of compassion, otherwise love is just a sterile thought or emotion.

By practicing compassion daily, you will build up this important spiritual virtue muscle, and more easily love others as God loves us. You will be freer to put your love into action, serving, forgiving, and calling others to treat each other with love and respect.

8

Prudence

"For which of you, desiring to build a tower, does not first sit down and count the cost, whether he has enough to complete it?"

—Luke 14:28

The virtue of prudence is the habit of making wise and healthy decisions and acting upon them. It is not about being prudish, indecisive, or overly cautious—that is a *false* view of prudence. Real prudence is about discernment before action. The virtue of prudence is needed to make decisions that are well thought-out, well-timed, and have both a good goal in mind and a good way of achieving that goal. Saint Thomas Aquinas called prudence "right reason in action".[1]

In many ways, *prudence* is what some might call "common sense", except that prudence is actually not that common. We do not always make wise decisions, let alone act on them. It is interesting that the Latin word for *prudence* means "foresight", or the ability to discern the effects or outcomes of a particular action before it happens. With this in mind, prudence is less about caution and more about being able to think through the effects of possible decisions and discern the right course of action.

While prudence is generally an intellectual virtue, because it deals with discernment, it also deals with decision. Once the possibilities are discerned, there must be a decision. The prudent person discerns well, and upon finding the proper course of action, makes a decisive and confident decision. If one were only to discern and never to decide and act, he would not be prudent. If a person decides and acts without discerning, he also would not be prudent.

Prudence is considered the "queen of the virtues", since it directs reason to participate with the will and calls forth the other virtues. This virtue on a practical level helps us make good decisions. On a deeper level, it helps us distinguish between good and evil, and virtuous and vicious acts. And, on the deepest and most important level, it helps us to discern the will of God.

A prudent person takes in the available data, carefully discerns the options, considers past experience, considers the possibilities, and then chooses the course of action and timing that is most likely to produce the desired outcome. And, he does all this in a way that does not compromise or challenge his moral principles.

A Corresponding Beatitude

Prudent people make difficult decisions that people trust. They navigate through challenging situations with grace and poise. Jesus proclaimed, "Blessed are the peacemakers, for they shall be sons of God" (Mt 5:9). What is the connection between peacemaking and prudence? Conflicts are often started or prolonged when people act rashly, while prudence counteracts rashness by encouraging people to think before they say or do anything that could cause more harm. Prudence asks, "Is the damage being caused by this conflict worth whatever could be gained by it?" and "What can be done to bring about a reconciliation?" Sometimes conflicts are caused by injustice, which is why Pope Paul VI famously said, "If you want peace, work for justice."[2] It is interesting to note that the pope addressed his words to "Men of thought! Men of Action!", in other words, prudent men. This is because prudent people are able to discern the actions that are needed to act justly toward others—in their families, in their societies, and in the world community of nations.

When peacemakers bring prudent words and actions into a tense situation, calming down all the people involved, they are doing a work of charity. Beloved Saint Pio stressed the important relationship between prudence and love. He said, "You must always have prudence and love. Prudence has the eyes; love has the legs. Love which has the legs would like to run to God, but its impulse to rush toward Him is blind and at times might stumble, if it were not guided by prudence which has the eyes. When prudence sees that love could become unbridled, it loans its eyes to love. In this way love restrains itself and, guided by prudence, acts as it should and not as it would like."[3]

Prudence and the Temperaments

Choleric

Alexandre Havard points out that prudence includes both "discernment and decision". People with a choleric temperament can be good at deciding. However, because they are motivated by action, they struggle with discernment, which necessarily takes time and patience.[4] Cholerics need to develop the virtue of prudence by making time for discernment. This means that the choleric person needs to practice gathering information, listening, analyzing the outcomes of different scenarios, and seeking the counsel of others before acting.

Sanguine

Sanguines also need to take the time needed for discernment. They tend to be overly optimistic and are generally open to adventure and activity. And they tend to make decisions based on feelings and the desire for excitement. This means that sanguines need to learn how to check their emotions while they gather information and seek good counsel. They often need to invite a friend they trust to help them with discernment.

Melancholic

The melancholic person, on the other hand, excels at discernment, as long as he does not overthink the issue. But he is challenged by making decisions. In fact, most melancholics would be happy to spend all of their time in discernment because they are fearful of making a bad decision. The graver the possibilities, the more fearful they are.

Phlegmatic

Phlegmatics excel at discernment. They can approach a decision relatively dispassionately and analytically, but they are not always comfortable making a decision. In fact, it can take almost heroic virtue for a phlegmatic to make a decision, especially on behalf of others.

They need to grow in the virtue of prudence by making decisions the moment they have completed their discernment.

Associated Virtues

The virtue of prudence is assisted and practiced more readily when accompanied by these other virtues.

- *Wisdom* is properly applying knowledge to a situation.
- *Understanding* is gaining knowledge about a situation.
- *Patience* is giving oneself time for adequate discernment and response.
- *Decisiveness* is responding appropriately and in a timely manner.
- *Orderliness* is prioritizing and organizing in a constructive way.

Associated Vices

- Rashness—acting without thinking through the consequences. *Steals your ability to enter into the discernment process and grow from it.*
- Cowardice—failing to initiate action or to stay the course because of "what ifs". *Steals your ability to learn through trial and error and to be proud of your actions.*
- Laziness—failing to give the situation the attention and the effort it deserves. *Steals your ability to use your particular gifts to serve others.*
- Pride—thinking too highly of yourself; failing to discern before taking action because you are more concerned about looking good and being right in your own eyes than doing the truly right thing. *Steals the true happiness that comes from making good decisions for the benefit of others instead of gratifying your own ego.*

Practical Ways to Grow

Now that we're finished with the textbook stuff, let's talk about prudence in action, and what it takes to develop this virtue at work, at home, and in life. To be prudent, you need to do four things:

1. Make time for discernment.
2. Set a reasonable deadline for making a decision.
3. Do that which you decide to do.
4. Evaluate the outcomes and learn from them.

Practice prudence in small things. Before eating a meal, think through its nutritional value, the portion size and calories, when your next meal might be, and so on. This should help guide your decisions about what, when, and how much you eat. When buying something, ask yourself, "Is this truly prudent? Do I need this thing? Do I need it now? Can I afford it?"

By practicing prudence daily, you will build up this important spiritual virtue muscle, and more easily choose the good in your life.

9

Justice

"Truly, I say to you, as you did it to one of the least of these
my brethren, you did it to me."

—Matthew 25:40

The virtue of justice is the habit of giving others what they are due.
For the Christian, it is giving to others gladly, for as Saint Paul said,
"God loves a cheerful giver" (2 Cor 9:7). The word *gladly* is really
important. The just Christian is not upset or begrudging about having to do what justice demands, rather he is happy to give God and
others what they deserve. Often, we think too narrowly of justice
as only retribution, that is, punishing someone for the wrong he has
done. But, in truth, justice goes beyond that, for it is motivated by
the desire to be in right relationship with others by treating them
with the respect their human dignity deserves. Real justice is tem-
pered with mercy. When someone rightfully deserves punishment,
we deliver justice in a way that advances his good as well as the
common good.

The Just Person

Saint Isidore, a patron saint of Western civilization, explained, "A righteous (*iustus*) person is so called because he keeps the laws (*ius*) and
lives according to the law."[1] Because people who practice the virtue of
justice are law-abiding, they are trustworthy and honorable, two traits
that every society needs. They hold themselves accountable, and they

hold others accountable by reminding them of what justice demands with clarity and charity.

We are wired to be upset by injustice. As the old saying goes: "Even a thief doesn't want his stuff stolen." But we must not want justice only for ourselves while committing injustices against others. As Martin Luther King Jr. said, "Injustice anywhere is a threat to justice everywhere."[2] To have a good society, we must follow the Golden Rule to treat others the way we want to be treated. This means acting justly, advancing justice for all, and protecting others from injustice.

While justice is gladly giving others their due and intervening to stop injustice, it does not mean being judge, jury, and executioner if those roles have not been assigned to us. Jesus said, "Judge not, that you be not judged" (Mt 7:1). We are not to avenge the wrongs committed against us but to seek justice through civil authorities.

When Christians are wronged, even as they seek justice from the proper authorities, they are asked to forgive those who have injured them. Jesus said, "For if you forgive men their trespasses, your heavenly Father also will forgive you, but if you do not forgive men their trespasses, neither will your Father forgive your trespasses" (Mt 6:14). Think for a moment of the basic Christian message. God is rich in mercy and quick to forgive those who are sorry and seek to do better, and He asks us to be like Him. After all, the entire Christian message is about God coming to save us with His mercy. Jesus came not to condemn the world but to save the world through the forgiveness of sins (Jn 3:17; Lk 1:77).

There is an old story that illustrates the patience of God toward sinners. A nomad was sitting outside his tent one evening, when he witnessed an old man wandering in the desert. He invited him in for a meal. The old man immediately began eating without first offering a prayer of thanksgiving to God. The host blurted out, "Do you not honor God?" To which the old man replied, "I do not believe in God and fend for myself." Furious, the host threw the old man out, seeking in justice to defend God's honor. That night in prayer, God asked him why he threw out the old man. He answered, "Because he dishonors You, Lord." To which God replied, "I've suffered that old man's dishonor for eighty years, could you not endure him patiently for even just one night?"

God sets before each of us this choice: we can either honor Him and others by being just *and* merciful, or we can judge others harshly. We can bless or curse; we should not do both. "From the same mouth come blessing and cursing. My brethren, this ought not to be so" (Jas 3:10). In choosing to bless, we can hold ourselves and others accountable to the truth. We can instruct the ignorant. We can pray for the obstinate. But we dare not lack mercy in how we deal out justice. "For judgment is without mercy to one who has shown no mercy" (Jas 2:13).

Justice in Scripture

Scripture constantly reminds us of the importance of justice. In the first book of the Bible, we are told "to keep the way of the LORD by doing righteousness and justice" (Gen 18:19). The Hebrew words here for "righteousness and justice" speak to both desiring justice and actively building a just world by following God's law. This term is used over and over again to describe King David, who was "a man after [God's] own heart" (1 Sam 13:14).

God is described as the truly just one: "He executes justice for the fatherless and the widow, and loves the sojourner, giving him food and clothing" (Deut 10:18). "Clouds and thick darkness are round about him; righteousness and justice are the foundation of his throne" (Ps 97:2). And God asks us to model our lives after His example: "Justice, and only justice, you shall follow, that you may live and inherit the land which the LORD your God gives you" (Deut 16:20). "Give justice to the weak and the fatherless; maintain the right of the afflicted and the destitute" (Ps 82:3).

Just people are in right relationship with God. "To do righteousness and justice is more acceptable to the LORD than sacrifice" (Prov 21:3). "Evil men do not understand justice, but those who seek the LORD understand it completely" (Prov 28:5). And just people lead good lives: "And if any one loves righteousness, her labors are virtues; for she teaches self-control and prudence, justice and courage; nothing in life is more profitable for men than these" (Wis 8:7).

Jesus came to establish justice by reminding us of who we are and reconciling us with God, with others, and with the land. The prophet Isaiah had foretold that this is what the Messiah would do: "Behold my servant, whom I uphold, my chosen, in whom my soul delights; I have put my Spirit upon him, he will bring forth justice to the nations" (Is 42:1). Believing Jesus was the promised Messiah, Matthew quoted this prophecy of Isaiah in his Gospel: "This was to fulfil what was spoken by the prophet Isaiah, 'Behold, my servant whom I have chosen, my beloved with whom my soul is well pleased. I will put my Spirit upon him, and he shall proclaim justice to the Gentiles'" (Mt 12:18).

To say that justice is a central theme of Scripture, and the basis for human society, is not an overstatement. It is for the sake of justice that we owe God our very lives. We give a portion of our labors to God as an offering because he has given us everything. It is for the sake of justice that we defend and protect others. It is for the sake of justice that we expect, rightly so, to be treated fairly and with respect. And it is for the sake of justice that we treat others the way we want to be treated by fulfilling our obligations and promises: we pay our workers what we agreed to pay them in a timely way because they deserve their wages; we tell the truth to others because they deserve the truth; and, we are faithful to our spouses as we promised we would be because they deserve our fidelity.

A just person seeks to be in right relationship with God and others. He knows that the foundation of all relationships is giving others what they are due. And this serves the common good, for a just society is a harmonious one, which is the reason Pope Saint Paul VI said, "If you want peace, work for justice."[3]

A Corresponding Beatitude

Jesus proclaimed, "Blessed are those who hunger and thirst for righteousness, for they shall be satisfied" (Mt 5:6). By using the terms "hunger" and "thirst", Jesus showed that justice is as necessary for us as food and water. He affirmed that those who seek justice will be satisfied because they not only will live better lives and help others do the same, but also will be rewarded by God. "Whatever your task, work heartily, as serving the Lord ... knowing that from the Lord you will receive the inheritance as your reward" (Col 3:23–24).

Some of our best employees and workers are men and women who simply and quietly do what is required of them and do so with joy. We often don't think of laziness as a form of injustice, but in fact it is shirking our responsibilities to our employers and our families. Laziness hinders our ability to place our strengths and talents at the service of others for the common good.

Many of the most acceptable vices are really forms of laziness. According to a Nielsen report, we spend almost six hours a day watching videos.[4] And the Barna Group found that 51 percent of all Americans seek out and view pornography and that 67 percent of young men and 33 percent of young women routinely view pornography.[5] Pornography use (note that the Greek word *pornē* means "prostitute") is not only a form of idleness but also an injustice to the person being viewed and used as an object for sexual gratification. Pornography is not only idleness but also lust.

Here are two other socially acceptable forms of injustice: greed and envy. We tend to assume that generosity goes hand in hand with making a lot of money, but paradoxically, the more money a person earns, the less of it he gives away as a percentage of his income. He often greedily keeps more of his wealth to himself instead of sharing it generously with others. The greedy person tends not to pay fairly those who work for him, and as the book of Sirach says, "To deprive an employee of his wages is to shed blood" (34:22). But people who complain that others make more or have more than they, are often guilty of envy. Having worked as a national advertising executive for twenty-five years, Tom knows well that advertising campaigns often rely on "benign envy" to entice people to buy products they don't really need and possibly can't really afford. Young social media users have indicated that envy is often one of the principal reactions they experience when they look at other people's posts. Envy is an affront to thankfulness; it is a failure to rejoice over the blessings and earnings of others.

Justice and the Temperaments

Choleric

People with a choleric temperament often understand the value of the common good, that which benefits the big picture of the society, the family, the business, and so on. However, because they are motivated by action, they may mistreat other people by making unfair demands. For them the mission or the goal tends to take priority over the well-being of others, and they may be tempted to use people as a means to their own ends. In seeking to serve the common good of their operation, they may run over the people they see as blocking their path.

In order to grow in the virtue of justice, cholerics need to think of how they are treating their employees and coworkers. They need to take the time to listen to them and to consider how they are supporting their particular talents. This means that the choleric person frequently needs to assess the emotions, the energy, and the workload of those they depend on and work with. They need to ask whether their mission and goal is noble, and whether they can achieve it in a way that builds up and supports those who are on mission with them.

Melancholic

Similar to the choleric, the melancholic person tends to see the ramifications of his actions as they relate to the common good. In fact, melancholics often excel at considering the effects of an idea on the common good, and often strive to serve the common good. However, they can be overly critical and tend not to play well with others. They can sometimes seem oblivious to the emotions, energy, and commitments of those they work with, not because they do not care about people, but because they tend to live more interiorly. The melancholic needs to practice the virtue of justice in similar ways to the choleric, by taking time to assess the emotions, needs, and attitudes of those around them.

Sanguine

In contrast, the sanguine temperament considers the emotions, energy, and commitment of others. However, because they are motivated by relationships, they tend not to consider the common good or the ramifications of their activity. There is an old joke about the sanguine who was so busy winning over his colleagues that he forgot where he was leading them. The sanguine needs to develop the virtue of justice by considering whether his activity is contributing to his primary vocation and other obligations. Justice demands that we fulfill our primary obligations first, and the sanguine can be unjust by sometimes forgetting what those are and losing sight of his true priorities.

Phlegmatic

Phlegmatics are peace-oriented and are often very sensitive to the demands of justice. They are excellent communicators and will listen and be attentive to those they are in relationship with. They also consider the common good and the ramifications of their activities and decisions. However, because they tend to avoid conflict, they may be passive and fail to advocate for justice. Phlegmatics must grow in the virtue of justice by boldly seeking the common good. They need to respond to injustice by calling others to behave as they should.

Associated Virtues

The virtue of justice is assisted and practiced more readily when accompanied by these other virtues.

- *Reverence/Piety* is justice toward God.
- *Commitment* is justice toward others.
- *Good Stewardship* is justice toward creation.
- *Honesty* is reverence for the truth and the truth that others deserve.
- *Industriousness* is using gifts and talents to provide for self and others.

Associated Vices

A lack of justice can manifest itself in many ways. To avoid injustice, we must avoid these vices.

- Greed—grasping material possessions beyond what you need. *Steals the ability to be thankful and satisfied.*
- Envy—resenting the possessions or the successes of others. *Steals the joy of being happy for others and sharing with others.*

- Lust—overindulging in sexual pleasure; failing to treat others with respect by using them as objects. *Steals the joy of intimate relationships and the goodness of the physical world, and makes it hard to receive your spouse as gift and to give yourself as gift.*
- Laziness—failing to give the situation the attention and the effort it deserves. *Steals the joy of being in relationship with others and growing in trust and friendship.*

Practical Ways to Grow

That's the textbook stuff but let us talk about real justice in action, and what it takes to develop this virtue at work, at home, and in life. To be just, a person needs to do four things:

1. Have a sincere desire for your family and friends to be treated with respect and become the men and women God made them to be.
2. Have a sincere desire for all people to know who they are and to live justly with one another.
3. Consistently evaluate your actions to see if they are honoring God and honoring your commitments.
4. Be willing to stand up against injustice, wherever and whenever you encounter it.

Practice justice in small things. Make God and your primary vocation the center of your life and the standard by which you judge success. Am I keeping the Lord's Day holy? And do I allow enough time for daily prayer and growing in relationship with God? After God, my next obligation is my family. Do I give enough of myself to my spouse and children? Do I spend enough time with them? Do I listen attentively to them? What about my employer? Am I putting in a full day's work? Am I developing my talents so that I can serve others better? How do behave toward coworkers, neighbors, and members of my community? Do I treat everyone I encounter with respect? Do I contribute to the well-being of society by fulfilling my civic responsibilities? Am I actively seeking to overcome injustice by my political involvement, and do I serve the poor by donating generously to worthy charities?

By practicing justice daily, you will build up this important spiritual virtue muscle, and you will more easily find joy in giving others what they are due. By practicing justice, you will also begin to go beyond justice, by having mercy and compassion. You will begin to see others as God sees them, as beloved sons and daughters, your brothers and sisters, who are worthy of your love, support, and sacrifice.

10

Self-Control

> "God did not give us a spirit of timidity but a spirit of power
> and love and self-control."
>
> —2 Timothy 1:7

The virtue of self-control (sometimes called temperance) helps you
to moderate your desire for pleasure so that you can make choices
that are good for you. With self-control you can easily say no to bad
things and yes to good things, and in the right amounts. And it helps
you to make these good choices gladly. Choosing gladly is really
important and may be hard at first. If we choose the good reluctantly or with regret, we aren't really strengthening this virtue. This is
why most diets fail. We choose the good food in the right portions
for a time, but we do so half-heartedly, looking forward to the day
when we will choose the food, or the amount of food, that is bad for
us. This is not full self-control; it's simply delayed gratification.

Real Self-Control

Real self-control goes beyond just delaying gratification or temporar-
ily saying no to things we know aren't good for us, though this can
be the start of forming this virtue. Often we think too narrowly of
self-control, seeing it as only saying no or denying ourselves of something we want. But self-control is bigger than this. It's about saying
yes to a greater good, a better way, that leads to a more real, full, and
nourishing life.

The virtue of self-control is about directing our passions and our desires toward what is good, beautiful, and true. Think about it, if you are challenged by gossiping, the first step will be biting your tongue and controlling what you say and how you say it. This is the saying–no part, and in truth it can be exhausting. But the real virtue of self-control is not just biting your tongue when you want to gossip, but saying yes to a better, more constructive way of speaking about others.

Self-Control and Freedom

People who practice the virtue of self-control have possession of their passions and desires. They do not repress or ignore their desires, rather they direct them toward the good. People with self-control are wise, strong, and know who they are. They have moved past just saying no to unhealthy desires and have matured to where they seek those things that contribute to their well-being, making them better people, better workers, better spouses, and so on. Self-control gives a person the freedom to act less impulsively.

If we give in to our impulses, that is, obey them without consulting our intellect—in other words, act without thinking—we often do stupid things. And we lose some of our freedom. How many times have we done something impulsively that we immediately regretted? Do this enough times, and the behavior becomes a bad habit, making it harder and harder to say no when we should. The person who cannot say no is the person without freedom. "The drunk who cannot refrain from drink is not a free person. No one would describe him as free. Only when he is capable of refusing the drink will he be free."[1] We could all use more self-control, more possession of our passions and desires, not so that we can destroy them, no, but so that we can be free to direct them toward what is truly good for us.

Most people think that we have only one of two options: totally give in, that is, become a slave to our desires or totally abstain and suppress our desires. The truth is that both of these options distort our freedom. We must align our will and our intellect to direct our passions and desires toward that which is best for us. It is true that sometimes we want and desire things that aren't good for us under any circumstances, and from these we must learn to abstain. But most of our desires are for good things; it's just that sin has distorted our desires so that we want too much of a good thing or a good thing at the wrong time.

Self-Control and Sexuality

Take for example our sexuality—a beautiful gift from our Creator through which we can participate with Him in making new "images of God" in this world. Sexuality is not bad, in fact, it is so good that it must be protected, revered, and set free to achieve the meaning and purpose God gave it—to unite a man and a woman in a faithful, lifelong marriage, and to bring new life into the world.

If our sexuality becomes about pleasure only or removes its unitive (joining two people together) and procreative (making babies) purpose within marriage, it becomes distorted and too small to fulfill us. People with self-control do not so much suppress their sexual appetite, as much as they choose to direct it toward something more true, beautiful, and good than instant and depersonalized gratification. They abstain from sex outside marriage, because they refuse to accept a degraded view of sexuality. They guard their chastity and seek to be pure in order to make a total and free gift of themselves to another person in marriage or to God exclusively in a religious calling.

Self-control in the sexuality department takes work and constant vigilance. It requires that we "take custody" of our eyes, which means choosing not to look at images that can excite disordered sexual desires. Once there was a father who was trying to teach his teenage son a lesson about avoiding harmful images. The son turned on the television and noticed a promo for a movie at eight o'clock. It had a rating of MA, meaning for mature audiences. The son said to his dad, "All the kids at school will be watching this movie, and their parents are going to let them watch it! I don't think I will even notice any of the bad parts of the movie. I can just ignore those parts and tune them out afterward." The dad replied, "We do not watch inappropriate movies in this house. A little bad mixed in can ruin the whole thing." But the son insisted that he could see the movie without any negative effects. So, the dad went into the kitchen to bake some brownies. Just before the movie was about to start, he handed the plate of brownies to his son, saying, "I need to warn you that a little dog poop got into the brownie batter. I do not think you'll even notice as it's mixed in really well." The son recoiled in disgust, saying, "I don't want to touch them! Why did you do that?" The father replied, "I didn't think you would mind. It's such a small amount, like the little bit of bad stuff in the movie you are about to watch." The son understood his father's analogy. A small amount of a bad ingredient can be enough to ruin something. Saint Paul used a similar analogy when he told the Galatians not to accept falsehood by saying, "A little leaven leavens all the dough" (Gal 5:9).

Having sexual self-control involves knowing your weaknesses, knowing what tempts you and leads you away from what is good, beautiful, and true. We must be on guard not to tempt ourselves, and we must be vigilant in seeing, consuming, and doing those things that are good for us. This is especially true with regard to the media we consume and the proliferation of graphic images and videos on the internet. There are several great internet filters and accountability programs to help empower you to say yes to a more pure and fulfilling life.

Not Just Saying No

It is worth repeating: self-control is not just about saying no; it is also about saying yes to being truly free to fulfill our natural desires in ways that build us up and bring true happiness. According to British playwright Joseph Addison, "Temperance [self-control] allows nature full play. With temperance, nature can exert herself in all her force and vigor."[2] With self-control we can direct our passions toward what they were made for.

Father Joseph Esper in his book Saintly Solutions explains that "God is able to provide us with all we need, and he wants us to enjoy the blessings of his creation, but we must do so in a balanced and reasonable way. Food, drink, clothing, shelter, and rest are necessary things, and seeking various other comforts and enjoyments can be quite legitimate. The failing of self-indulgence, however, occurs when we give these things higher priority than we give the will of God."[3]

Self-indulgence is a fault we must work to overcome by growing in the virtue of self-control. Through practice, we must train ourselves to say no to harmful things, so that we are free to say yes to better, more noble things. These more noble things are exactly those blessings of creation that God knows will truly bring us lasting peace and true happiness.

Saint Catherine of Siena said, "Ponder the fact that God has made you a gardener, to root out vice and plant virtue."[4] Self-control is precisely the virtue we need to root out the weeds of impulsive behaviors and to replace them with good habits that bring life and true joy. Saying yes to better and more life-giving choices does indeed mean denying ourselves and saying no to the choices that harm us and others. At first this may feel like a burden. We all have bad habits that rob our peace and steal our joy, and we all struggle with self-control. But the struggle is worth it.

Alexandre Havard explains that the virtue of self-control requires both "energizing noble passions and subduing evil passions".[5] Both aspects are required: empowering, strengthening, and forming our noble passions—those desires that make us most fully alive—and admitting, calling out, and subduing distorted passions. The noble passion for freedom must be energized, while the evil passion of licentiousness (doing whatever we want without considering the consequences) must be subdued. The noble passion for relationship and making a gift of ourselves to others must be encouraged and strengthened. In turn, the evil passion of using others for our enjoyment must be subdued. The noble passion for life and sustenance must be strengthened and formed wisely, whereas the evil passion for overconsumption and overindulgence must be subdued. The noble passion for sensory pleasure and awe that draws our hearts toward what is beautiful must be cultivated, yet the evil passion for self-pleasure through quick and easy self-gratification must be subdued. The noble passion for work and leaving a legacy in this world must be formed and reinforced, but the evil passion for laziness on one hand and reckless busyness on the other must be subdued. This list could go on and on. The point is that self-control is about saying yes to the truth of who we are and what we were made for and saying no to those cheap, false, and distorted imitations that will never fulfill us.

In chapter 2 we discussed Father Spitzer's Four Levels of Happiness. Level one comes from sensory pleasures. While these are often good, they are insufficient to provide true happiness. The person who lives only for pleasure is not truly living at all. The virtue of self-control frees us from living only for pleasure and liberates our hearts to desire the higher goods that bring lasting joy.

Self-Control in Scripture

Scripture teaches the importance of self-control and shows how growth in this virtue requires both our effort and God's grace. Jesus said that we must take up our crosses and follow Him (see Mt 16:24–26), and He gave us the perfect example of self-denial to follow. He came that we "may have life and have it abundantly" (Jn 10:10), and this means accepting the help of His grace to choose the good gifts of God over the counterfeits offered by the world. He said, "Be perfect as your heavenly Father is perfect" (Mt 5:48) and "Seek first his kingdom and his righteousness, and all these things shall be yours as well" (Mt 6:33). And He died and rose from the dead to give us the grace to do so. His entire life and teaching serve as both a guide and a source for living in the knowledge of who we truly are and denying ourselves harmful pleasures so that we can be open to the new life He offers.

Both Saint Peter and Saint Paul were confident that living in the grace of Christ strengthened their own efforts to grow in self-control. Peter said, "Make every effort to supplement your faith with virtue, and virtue with knowledge, and knowledge with self-control, and self-control with steadfastness, and steadfastness with godliness, and godliness with brotherly affection, and brotherly affection with love" (2 Pet 1:5–7). Saint Paul explained the importance of self-control in the Christian life, reminding us that "God did not give us a spirit of timidity but a spirit of power and love and self-control" (2 Tim 1:7). He also encouraged us by saying, "No temptation has overtaken you that is not common to man. God is faithful, and he will not let you be tempted beyond your strength, but with the temptation will also provide the way of escape, that you may be able to endure it" (1 Cor 10:13). He said, "Do you not know that your body is a temple of the Holy Spirit within you, which you have from God? You are not your own; you were bought with a price. So glorify God in your body" (1 Cor 6:19–20).

During the early years of the Church, Corinth held the Isthmian Games, an ancient sports competition similar to the Olympics, which included track and field, wrestling, and boxing. Paul used the games to explain the virtue of self-control to the Corinthians: "Do you not know that in a race all the runners compete, but only one receives the prize? So run that you may obtain it. Every athlete exercises self-control in all things. They do it to receive a perishable wreath, but we an imperishable. Well, I do not run aimlessly, I do not box as one beating the air; but I pommel my body and subdue it, lest after preaching to others, I myself should be disqualified" (1 Cor 9:24–27).

Saint Paul understood the relationship between self-control and freedom, and the difference between freedom and licentiousness, "For you were called to freedom, brethren; only do not use your freedom as an opportunity for the flesh, but through love be servants of one another" (Gal 5:13). We all need self-control in order to have the freedom to become our true selves. Each person will struggle in different ways, and the training for each of us will look a little different, but the goal is the same: to participate in the plan of God to become like Him.

A Corresponding Beatitude

People who have self-control have pure hearts. They are honest with themselves, and they gladly choose those things that make them more alive, more holy, and more capable of loving God and others. People trust people with self-control because they know they will not be used or abused by them. They look to them as models of virtue and self-possession. People with self-control do not often raise their voice, they do not gossip, they do not overindulge in food or drink, they do not seek after worldly things or worldly approval. They are not naysayers or killjoys, but they are inspiring people who are humble and strong and single-hearted in their desire to treat others well and to serve God with great confidence and joy.

Jesus proclaimed, "Blessed are the pure in heart, for they shall see God" (Mt 5:8). He meant that those who know who they truly are in relationship to God and seek to please Him in all they do, can see Him as He truly is: the heavenly Father who loves them and wants what is best for them. The greater our confidence in the goodness of God's will for us, the more able we are to make a gift of ourselves to Him, and the more we come to realize that He is cheering for us to reach the finish line. He wants us to be happy with Him in this life and in the next, *for eternity*! When we cling to this truth, we have greater self-control when faced with temptation. Said another way, the more we aim for heaven, the more our circumstances in this world make sense, and the more we can see God at work in our lives, even in our trials. As Saint Paul said, "We know that in everything God works for good with those who love him, who are called according to his purpose" (Rom 8:28). He also said, "God is for us" (Rom 8:31).

When our hearts are divided we have a harder time with self-control. Jesus said, "No one can serve two masters; for either he will hate the one and love the other, or he will be devoted to the one and despise the other. You cannot serve God and mammon" (Mt 6:24). And what is "mammon"? It's wealth, and the comforts it can provide, which can become a rival to God. Bombarded by images of the supposed good life, it is easy to believe that gourmet food, designer clothes, luxurious homes, and hotspot vacations are the primary goals in life. The idea of voluntarily cutting back on what we consume in order to live a simpler life more centered on God, strikes some people as practically un-American.

American Catholics were once more familiar with the idea that self-denial in the forms of generous almsgiving, daily prayer, and regular fasting were ways of making us more detached from the things of this world and more free and alive in God. This is the real good life—knowing who you are and growing into that person more and more each day. We do that by cultivating the virtue of self-control so that we can make the sometimes difficult choices to become a better spouse, parent, and so on. Pope Benedict said, "The ways of the Lord are not easy, but we were not created for an easy life, but for great things, for goodness."[6] Indeed, being self-controlled is not easy.

It is not easy to deny oneself. It is not easy to say no to some of the things we want. But it is easier to say yes to better, greater, and more meaningful things. Saint Columban once said, "Humility makes you strong, denying yourself makes you Christlike."[7]

Self-Control and the Temperaments

Choleric

People with a choleric temperament have lots of energy to achieve their noble aspirations because they are motivated by action and results. They can enthusiastically say yes to challenges and are energized by achieving the goal. However, this activism can often blind them to their evil passions, and they can often be aggressive, angry, and easily provoked. Cholerics often need to check their pride, anger, judgment, and assumptions about others. They need to work hard at neither getting angry at others who work at a different pace nor questioning their tactics or motives. They need to avoid assuming the worst of others, especially those who question them. They need to grow in self-control over their pride, anger, aggression, and judgments by thinking the best of others until proven otherwise. They need to control the volume of their voice and to argue for their position without dominating others. They can do this by taking the time to ask others for their opinions and to listen to them attentively.

Melancholic

Similar to the choleric, the melancholic person usually does not struggle with fulfilling their noble aspirations. They want to serve the common good, and they admire others who share this ambition. However, they can be prone to pessimism and doubt, and they are often overly critical of themselves and others. They may doubt that they are capable of overcoming challenges or that others have access to the grace that can assist them in their struggle. Many melancholics suffer from sadness and anxiety, which, if left unchecked, can lead to more serious depression. The melancholic needs to practice the virtue of self-control by growing in confidence and trusting in God, themselves, and others. They need to temper their pessimism with the view that things might actually work out well. They need to practice supporting and encouraging others while still offering their insights and thoughts.

Sanguine

Similarly, the sanguine temperament also has plenty of energy for their noble passions; but because they are more motivated by their senses, they struggle with subduing their appetites. This can be one of the most persistent struggles for a sanguine. Physical pleasure, fun experiences, and so on often dominate their desires, which, if left unchecked, can quickly lead them further away from their responsibilities. Sanguines need to learn self-control over their senses. They need to guard against sights, sounds, tastes, and feelings that could lead them into temptation, while cultivating their appreciation for good things in the right amounts. They need to work on eating nourishing food in healthy portions, surrounding themselves with friends who can hold them accountable, and selecting entertainments (films, music, and books) that inspire noble desires.

Phlegmatic

Phlegmatics are peace-oriented and tend to have an analytic streak that allows them to approach reality without emotions clouding their view. They excel at subduing evil inclinations. They can easily say no to things that do not contribute to bringing peace to others and themselves. They tend to stay calm under pressure and are not prone to anger or anxiety. However, because they tend to avoid conflict, they are often passive with respect to their higher aspirations. They may hesitate to take risks and to stretch themselves to obtain a great good. The phlegmatic may feel that since he is not a horrible person, he does not need to work on becoming a better person. For this reason, phlegmatics must grow in the virtue of self-control by challenging themselves to greatness. They must push themselves out of their complacency to want true peace, which is not just the lack of conflict, but the full harmony that is achieved when everyone becomes who he is meant to be.

Associated Virtues

The virtue of self-control is assisted and practiced more readily when accompanied by these other virtues.

- *Custody of emotions* is directing emotions toward what is good.
- *Custody of senses* is directing senses (sight, hearing, taste) toward what is good.
- *Custody of the tongue* is speaking the truth in love and avoiding deception, detraction, slander, and gossip.
- *Custody of imagination* is directing our thoughts toward what is good, true, and beautiful.
- *Listening* is paying attention to your thoughts and feelings and taking time to listen to other people.
- *Chastity* is moderating the desire for sexual pleasure according to what is good and appropriate in your state in life.
- *Modesty* is showing respect for yourself and others by the way you talk, act, and dress.

Associated Vices

A lack of self-control can manifest itself in the following vices:

- Greed—grasping material possessions beyond what you need; willingness to gain at the expense of others by depriving them of what they need or deserve. *Steals one's ability to be thankful and satisfied.*
- Gluttony—overindulging in the pleasures of food and drink. *Steals the joy of choosing the good in the right amount and being satisfied by it.*
- Envy—resenting the possessions or the successes of others. *Steals the joy of being thankful for what you have and of being happy for others.*
- Lust—overindulging in sexual pleasure; failing to treat others with respect by using them as objects. *Steals the joy of intimate relationships and the goodness of the physical world. Makes it hard to receive your spouse as gift and to give yourself as gift.*

- Laziness—failing to give the situation the attention and the effort it deserves. *Steals the joy of using one's talents for the benefit of oneself and others.*

Practical Ways to Grow

That's the textbook stuff, but let us talk about real self-control in action, and what it takes to develop this virtue at work, at home, and in life. To have self-control, a person needs to do five things:

1. Know yourself and be honest about your struggles.
2. Be aware of your physical and emotional needs and discipline yourself to fulfill them appropriately. For example, when you are hungry you take the trouble to prepare nutritious food rather than waiting until you are so hungry that you binge on junk food.
3. Take daily steps to have small victories in subduing your evil passions and energizing your noble passions.
4. Ask others for help in overcoming your vices.
5. Trust in God's mercy, and His desire for you to grow in self-control.

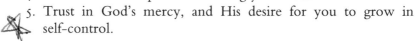

Rome wasn't built in a day, and saints aren't made overnight. Remember God's loving mercy, and give yourself some mercy, too, especially when the evil one keeps accusing you of some repetitive fault, failing, or sin.

Practice self-control by denying yourself a small pleasure or fasting or abstaining from small things. For example, say no to sugar in your coffee or forego a meal and give the money you would have spent to a homeless person or charity. Abstaining from meat every Friday used to be normative for Catholics. Now that practice is required only on Ash Wednesday, the Fridays of Lent, and Good Friday. But many Catholics are finding that abstaining from meat all the Fridays of the year is a good discipline for growing in self-control. Same for fasting—Catholics are obliged to fast only on Ash Wednesday and Good Friday, but many people, and not just Catholics, are discovering the physical, mental, and emotional benefits of regular fasting. There are many ways to fast, but essentially it means to go without food for a period of time, whether for a day or for so many hours in a day.

Abstaining from media for a period of time, by saying no to films or television shows, the internet or social media, and so on, is also a great way to deny yourself something and to replace it with something better, like volunteering, learning a hobby, or getting more exercise. All of these things make us feel good, and the better we feel, the more we are able to practice self-control.

The acronym H.A.L.T., which stands for *hungry, angry, lonely, or tired*, calls to mind that we are affected by many things. Many failures in self-control come when we are physically or emotionally weakened, which is when we need to be extra vigilant against temptations to do things we know we should avoid. We do not need a peer-reviewed study to convince us that when we are hungry, angry, lonely, or tired we are more likely to fail. The devil tempts us most when we are vulnerable, because the devil wants us to fail. Thus, when we are hungry, angry, lonely, or tired, we must halt, pause, before making a decision in order to avoid falling for a temptation.

Don't be afraid to ask for help. Seek a spiritual director or at least an accountability partner with whom you can share your struggles. Such mentors have likely faced challenges similar to your own. Consider what would happen if you told a trusted coworker, "I am really struggling with gossip and trying to work on it, would you do me a favor and hold me accountable when I'm at work? If I start to gossip or encourage others to gossip, will you let me know, and help me grow in this area?" Most coworkers would appreciate your honesty and be honored with the trust you have in them.

Even lust and gluttony can be subdued by asking the help of your friends or spouse. For serious addiction, be honest, and seek the help of a Christian professional. Find a good Catholic or other Christian counselor who knows what the Lord asks of us, and work with that person to grow in self-control. Another approach is a twelve-step program or one of the more recently developed online accountability programs.

Remember that self-control, like all the virtues, comes from repeated practice with the help of God's grace. Don't forget to pray and to receive frequently the Sacraments of Eucharist and Reconciliation as you work at strengthening your resolve. During a confession a man asked an elderly priest, "Does it get any easier?" To the man's surprise the priest said, "No!" At which point the man felt a little crestfallen. The priest continued, "No, but you will get stronger and be able to carry your cross more joyfully." The man left inspired and renewed. He told himself that he is getting stronger, that his sins do not define him. It is the practice and the discipline of good habits, including the habits of receiving the sacraments, that help us to overcome our bad habits.

By practicing self-control daily, you will build up this important spiritual virtue muscle. As you regain your freedom, you will experience the joy of saying no to the bad things in order to say yes to the good things God desires for you in this life. You will begin to discover new passions and new talents that will help you to grow more and more into the person God has made you to be and the person you want to be.

Courage

"Be strong and of good courage, do not fear or be in dread . . .
for it is the LORD our God who goes with you; he will not fail
you or forsake you."

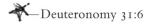—Deuteronomy 31:6

The virtue of courage (sometimes called fortitude) is the habit of
bravely responding to what each situation demands. In many ways
this is the easiest virtue to understand. We all know what courage
looks like—a brave man or woman responding to a crisis with great
conviction, overcoming fear and doing what the situation demands,
and never giving up. We admire courage and cheer whenever we
hear about the firefighter who dashes into the burning building to
save a child, the soldier who runs back under fire to rescue his fallen
comrade, the corporate executive who gives up his career to care for
a sick spouse, and so on. But it is just as courageous to say no to a
promotion that will cause you many more nights at work, in order
to be more present to your family. It is also courageous to choose
life and bring a child into the world, despite difficult circumstances.
Courage may be one of the most attractive virtues, because it shows
the well-formed will in action.

We also all know what courage is not. It is neither cowardice nor
rashness. Cowardice is the refusal to do what a dangerous or incon-
venient situation demands because of fear. We have all heard stories
about people who had the chance to do the right thing and failed to
do it because of fear, or worse, did a terrible thing instead, as when
men on the *Titanic* took life jackets from children or dressed as
women in order to get themselves into the lifeboats. We find their

cowardice despicable, and so we should. Rashness, on the other hand, is brazenly ignoring fear in the face of danger and acting reck-lessly, often while needlessly putting even more people in danger, as when a commanding officer rushes with his troops into a firefight against all warning that they will accomplish nothing and likely die, and many of them are killed. In both cases, cowardice and rashness, the person is reacting emotionally and not acting rationally.

Our Own Battles

Think of one particular battle in your life; it can be big or small. Maybe the battle you are thinking of is staying up too late, not exercising enough, eating too much, spending too much time with social or other media, or being annoyed by a family member or coworker. Maybe what comes to mind is something more serious, something related to a failure to fulfill a commitment. As mentioned in the first chapter, there are four ways you can engage your battle. You can ignore it, you can medicate and distract yourself from it, you can confront your prob-lem unequipped, or you can confront your problem well equipped. Options one and two are cowardice, option three is brazenness, and option four is real courage, entering the battle well equipped.

Every day of your life includes dealing with little battles, and if these are engaged with courage they can be looked at as training for bigger battles—not training necessarily in the technical sense, but in a general sense. When we confront small challenges we strengthen our sense of right and wrong, our willingness to accept challenges, and our confidence that God is with us. When faced with a crisis, brave people can act courageously because, little did they know it, they had been training themselves for a big battle with every smaller one they refused to ignore. To be courageous in the big things, we need to be courageous in a thousand little ways beforehand.

Several hidden-camera TV shows focus on how people react to a staged crisis or event. One episode from *The Steve Harvey Show* staged a fight between a couple that would appear as a case of domestic abuse. Most bystanders sat idly by, and one couple even asked to be moved so that they did not have to hear the troubling conversation. One man, clearly older and smaller than the intimidating boyfriend, intervened by telling the young woman that she did not have to put up with his abuse and that he would protect her. He wasn't a trained counselor, a cop, or a black belt in karate. He was a grandfather who knew that the situation demanded action. He didn't train for this situation in the technical sense, but he was equipped in the general sense and had developed the virtue of courage.[1]

The Courageous Person

People who practice the virtue of courage have wills strongly linked to their sense of right and wrong. They respond prudently to challenges. They are not motivated by the fear of doing the wrong thing, but by the fear of not doing anything at all. People who are courageous are not necessarily bold (that depends very much on their temperament), but they are brave; they have stout hearts. The virtue of courage helps people to do the right thing, at the right time, for the right reason.

Alexandre Havard points out that courage has both *audacity*, a willingness to take risks and hope for great things, and *perseverance*, the energy to stay the course. It means never giving up.[2] Said another way, courage is about both initiating action and sustaining it despite the challenges. As Aristotle said, "The brave man endures and acts as courage directs."[3] We would not consider a person who runs to the battle but cannot stay for the fight to be a person of courage. Nor would we consider courageous a person who waits for the last moment to engage in battle and then takes some of the credit for the victory. True courage has both audacity and perseverance.

Fear

Courage is not the absence of fear but the will to do the right thing in spite of it. Saint Ignatius of Loyola, the soldier turned saint, said, "God's love calls us to move beyond fear. We ask God for the courage to abandon ourselves unreservedly, so that we might be molded by God's grace, even as we cannot see where that path may lead us."[4] Mark Twain said, "Courage is resistance to fear, mastery of fear—not absence of fear."[5] Nelson Mandela said it in similar words: "I learned that courage was not the absence of fear, but the triumph over it. The brave man is not he who does not feel afraid, but he who conquers that fear."[6] This insight is important.

Our doubts about who we are, what we are capable of, and whether we will become the person our families need and God wants us to be are born from fear: fear of failure, fear of pain, fear of being forgotten, and so on. The virtue of courage is about mastering fear and self-doubt. It is about not believing the lies we are told by the evil one, lies meant to discourage and paralyze us, and not succumbing to them. Courage is trusting that God can and will work through us and is glad to do so. Jesus said, "Fear not, little flock, for it is your Father's good pleasure to give you the kingdom" (Lk 12:32). Saint Faustina's Divine Mercy painting of Jesus features the powerful words *Jezu Ufam Tobie* (Jesus, I trust in You!)

Courage in the Scriptures

The most common phrases in Scripture are "Be not afraid" and similar assurances. They are repeated hundreds of times throughout both the Old and the New Testaments. (Some scholars have counted 366 times in Scripture, one for each day of the year and an extra one for leap years.) The words remind us that the Lord calls us not to have a spirit of cowardice but a deep trust in Him and His confidence in us. Pope Saint John Paul II said these words repeatedly as he inspired people to stand up against the injustices of Communism.

Here are some Old Testament examples. When the Lord appeared to Abraham, He said, "Fear not, Abram, I am your shield; your reward shall be very great" (Gen 15:1). God also told Isaac, Jacob, and Joseph not to fear. When Pharaoh's army pursued the newly freed Israelites, they cried to the Lord, and Moses said to them, "Fear not, stand firm, and see the salvation of the LORD, which he will work for you today" (Ex 14:13). The beloved Psalm 23 reminds us that God is near us whenever we face danger: "Even though I walk through the valley of the shadow of death, I fear no evil; for you are with me; your rod and your staff, they comfort me" (v. 4). With Psalm 56 we can say, "When I am afraid, I put my trust in you. In God, whose word I praise, in God I trust without a fear. What can flesh do to me?" (vv. 3–4).

The call to courage continues in the New Testament. The angel Gabriel said to Mary, "Do not be afraid" (Lk 1:30), and an angel told Joseph, "Do not fear" (Mt 1:20). Jesus told the apostles not to fear their mission. "Do not be afraid; henceforth you will be catching men" (Lk 5:10). To the leaders of the synagogue who didn't understand Him, Jesus said, "Do not fear, only believe" (Mk 5:36). To tell us about the Father's providential care, Jesus said, "Fear not, therefore; you are of more value than many sparrows" (Mt 10:31). Death is what we often fear most, and what did Jesus say about that? "Do not fear those who kill the body but cannot kill the soul; rather fear him who can destroy both soul and body in hell" (Mt 10:28). In other words, we have only one thing to fear: God, and rejecting His incredible love for us. When Scripture tells us to fear God, it is calling us to respect the Lord, the Almighty, as well as reminding us that the loss of heaven that comes from rejecting God is worse than death.

A Corresponding Beatitude

Christians with the virtue of courage know whom they serve and can suffer confidently and joyfully the persecution that sometimes comes from doing the will of God. It takes courage to say no to the lies and the false promises of the devil that drive many ambitions in our fallen world. It takes courage to stand up for the truth, because often defenders of the truth are persecuted, misunderstood, or rejected by those who have accepted a false vision of themselves and the purpose of this world.

A prominent university administrator left his job at an Ivy League school because he felt strongly that education should not be limited to the elite, but available for everyone who could benefit from a college education. To the astonishment of his colleagues, Michael M. Crow left Columbia University to become the president of Arizona State University. Even though the move was a promotion, some saw it as a step down to exchange East Coast prestige and privilege for a public school in Arizona. They could not understand Crow's desire to advance the good of common people west of the Hudson River. He wasn't angry with those who chided him; he was thankful for the experiences and the battles that had prepared him for his mission.

After eighteen years of serving public higher education, he has left an indelible mark on what a state university can be.

Courage comes in all shapes and sizes, but it is always about doing the right thing, at the right time, for the right reason, *and with the right attitude*. Courageous people of faith are remarkably humble—they are honest about their achievements and take proper pride in them, but they give glory to God by thanking and praising Him for how He worked through them. When Elizabeth said to Mary, "Blessed are you among women", Mary replied, "My soul magnifies the Lord" (Lk 1:42, 46) and then listed the mighty and merciful things God does. It takes courage to do God's will when it is something difficult and will meet with misunderstanding and opposition.

Jesus proclaimed, "Blessed are those who are persecuted for righteousness' sake, for theirs is the kingdom of heaven" (Mt 5:10). When we act righteously we participate in the life of God and already have one foot, so to speak, in His kingdom. With every right action, we bring God's healing to the brokenness of this world. How beautiful it is when people of faith have the courage to do difficult or even dangerous righteous acts. They show us what we are capable of doing with God's power.

Saint Teresa of Calcutta was a truly courageous person. She knew who she was and what God was asking her to do. Her mission was simple: to love Jesus in His distressing disguise of the poorest of the poor. Mother Teresa was misunderstood by many people; she was persecuted by those who thought her work was meaningless or who thought her faith was a threat. And she suffered a dark night of the soul, a loss of feeling God's love and closeness, that lasted many years. Yet she showed great audacity and perseverance in loving those who others thought were unlovable in some of the worst slums of the world.

Mother Teresa's courage has called countless others to take courage and to follow her example. Although only five feet tall, she was a powerful figure and presence, who bravely called others, including the most powerful, to live in right relationship with God and with others. The order she founded, the Missionaries of Charity, continues her work all over the world. From her letters, we learn that she struggled with doubt, anger, and even with depression. Despite those things, she had a deep trust in the Lord that He would provide all the strength she needed to do His will.

Having courage makes you freer to respond well to the challenges in your life. The difficulties we face are what forge us into the men and women God intends us to be. In hundreds of small ways each day, God is constantly giving us opportunities to grow in courage. These small battles and victories are what prepare us for whatever bigger battles may come. In the Sermon on the Mount, Jesus described the person who hears and responds to His word as "a wise man who built his house upon the rock; and the rain fell, the floods came, and the winds blew and beat upon that house, but it did not fall, because it had been founded on the rock" (Mt 7:24–25). Jesus did not say the house would stand *if* the rain fell. The rain falls on all of us. We experience floods in life. The winds blow, and our hearts shake. It is the virtue of courage that helps us to weather bravely whatever storms may come, confident that God's love, mercy, and power are at work in us.

Courage and the Temperaments

Choleric

People with a choleric temperament have lots of energy and courage. They can both initiate action and run the course for a long time. They are inclined to action so the challenges of life are seen as opportunities for engagement and training. The choleric's courage is part of his biology and not yet a virtue until it is directed by prudence and justice. A quote often, but mistakenly, attributed to Winston Churchill summarizes this well: "Courage is what it takes to stand up and speak. Courage is also what it takes to sit down and listen."[7] To have courage and not just activism, the choleric needs to discern and to practice doing the right thing, at the right time, for the right reason, and with the *right attitude*.

Melancholic and Phlegmatic

People who are melancholic or phlegmatic can endure much. They have firm wills and tend to be more stable and consistent than the other two temperaments. They have a lot of energy to endure the challenges of arriving at a conclusion or resolution. However, they are reserved and averse to taking risks. The melancholic temperament struggles with fear and tends to inflate challenges, while the phlegmatic temperament would rather accept the status quo and avoid rocking the boat. Both the melancholic and the phlegmatic need to practice audacity by boldly and prudently taking needed risks.

Sanguine

The sanguine is open to adventure and has lots of energy to initiate action but often lacks the ability to follow through with a plan when difficulties arise. Sanguines are prone to distraction and superficiality. Sensitive to pain and uncomfortable with conflict, they are easily tempted to compromise their convictions in order to be liked or to fit in with their group. They tend to put their energy and passion into whichever project or challenge is most recent. Sanguines can start hundreds of projects with ease, but they require effort and virtue to finish them. They need to develop the virtue of courage by working at perseverance. They need to learn to enjoy the entire process of a project, including the overcoming of challenges, and not the just the fun of starting a new thing.

Associated Virtues

The virtue of courage is assisted and practiced more readily when accompanied by these other virtues.

- ○ *Hope* is trust that the ultimate outcome will be worth any struggle to achieve it, and for the Christian, trust that God will provide whatever is needed to do His will.
- ○ *Grit/Determination* is firmness of purpose to see something through to the end.
- ○ *Patience/Long-Suffering* is willingness to endure hardships and pain for the sake of a greater good or mission.

Associated Vices

A lack of courage can manifest itself in many ways and we must be careful of these vices if we lack courage.

- Cowardice—being afraid of suffering or in anguish over the unknown such that you refuse to do what a situation demands. *Steals your ability to engage in noble battles and the joy of suffering for worthy causes.*
- Despair—lacking the hope that God will provide whatever you need to do His will. *Steals your ability to use your particular gifts to serve yourself and others.*
- Laziness—failing to give the situation the attention and the effort it deserves. *Steals the joy of being in right relationship with God, family members, employers, and coworkers.*

Practical Ways to Grow

That's the textbook stuff, but let's talk for a moment about real courage in action, and what it takes to develop this virtue at work, at home, and in life. To have courage, a person needs to do four things:

1. Admit that you will face challenges any time you try to do the right thing. *hard things*
2. Be willing to suffer for the sake of doing God's will.
3. Decide prudently which battles to fight.
4. Ask God for help and give glory to God for your victories.

Practice courage in the small things. Consider the battles in your life and ask yourself what does victory in that battle look like? Jesus said, "if your right hand causes you to sin, cut it off" (Mt 5:30). Luckily, He doesn't mean physical mutilation, but He does mean courageous action. If your smart phone leads you to sin, cut it off by getting a non-data plan or turning it off whenever it causes distractions or temptations. God wants us to be free of the vices that steal our joy. He does not want us to be afraid of them, but to fear that they may lead us away from the one thing that matters most—Him.

Remember that courage, like all the virtues, comes from repeated practice while receiving from God the grace we need. Listen to God's word, and let it sink in: "Be not afraid." God will help you any time you ask.

By practicing courage daily, you will build up this important spiritual muscle, and you will more easily find joy by engaging in the small and large battles you face. You will be freer and more prepared to do the right thing, in the right way, at the right time, with the right attitude, and you will rejoice with God who led you to victory.

12

Humility

"The fear of the LORD is instruction in wisdom, and humility goes before honor."

—Proverbs 15:33

The virtue of humility is the habit of living in the truth of who you are, knowing your strengths and weaknesses. It requires being honest with yourself. Some people think that humility means thinking little of oneself. In comparison with God, yes, we are very small. But truth demands that we also recognize our own dignity and giftedness as creatures of God, as well as the talents we have and the talents we have yet to cultivate. Some of the best musicians and authors have great humility: while they know they are good at what they do, they also know that they have room to grow.

Your Talents

Think for a moment of your own natural talents. Maybe you have always been good at music, math, problem solving, or listening to others. Maybe these things come more easily to you than to other people, and yet to become really good at them has taken some practice. God has given you these gifts, and He deserves thanks and praise for them.

Now think for a moment of talents you have had to work very hard at developing. Maybe you have spent long hours overcoming a speech impediment, learning a new language, or mastering a paintbrush. These gifts also come from God, of course, but their development was the result of a lot of hard work.

Maybe there are talents you admire in others, wish you had, but have not been able to acquire. Perhaps dancing doesn't come naturally to you; you have tried many times to develop the ability but find that you lack rhythm. Perhaps as a result you appreciate the ability of others to dance beautifully. Praise God for the weaknesses that allow you to accept that you cannot be great at everything and must depend on and appreciate those who have the talents you lack. Doing so, while acknowledging your strengths, is humility.

Pride

The virtue of humility is indispensable for counteracting the deadly sin of pride. Pride is too much esteem for ourselves. When we are proud, we assume that we can develop ourselves or our talents by our own unaided efforts, as so-called self-made men and women. We think that we can know what we want to know and do what we want to do without help from anyone else. Pride inflates our ego such that we think so highly of ourselves that we look down on others, assuming we are better than they are. We focus on the defects of others in order to feel superior to them. In its deadliest form, pride causes us to deny our dependence on God and our obligation to thank, praise, and obey Him.

Imagine our pride from God's perspective. He gives us everything. He gives us our very lives, our very next breath, not to mention our gifts and abilities. He gives us our families and all the other people who help us and inspire us to develop and to use our talents. He gives us a guardian angel to protect us and to nudge us in the right direction. When we go astray, God is quick to forgive. He allows us to learn from our mistakes, bringing good out of them. After a lifetime of God's paternal love, not one person, not one, could honestly say, "I have done everything on my own."

Humility in Scripture

We all know the proverb: "Pride goes before a fall." It comes from the Bible: "Pride goes before destruction, and a haughty spirit before a fall (Prov 16:18). Both the devil and our first parents fell because of pride and so do we. That is why the Scriptures urge us to be humble: "My son, glorify yourself with humility" (Sir 10:28). This command is even more important for the smart and gifted and strong of this world: "The greater you are, the more you must humble yourself; so you will find favor with God" (Sir 3:18). The fact is, when we fail to humble ourselves, to live in the truth about ourselves, we forget who we are—sons and daughters of God—and we turn away from Him.

Saint Augustine said, "It was pride that changed angels into dev-ils: it is humility that makes men as angels."[1] To call us back to the truth about ourselves, and to Himself, God set us the perfect example of humility: "Though he was in the form of God, [Jesus] did not count equality with God a thing to be grasped, but emptied himself, taking the form of a servant, being born in the likeness of men. And being found in human form he humbled himself and became obedient unto death, even death on a cross" (Phil 2:6–8). Jesus undid the knot of pride, and the resulting rebellion against God, through the Cross. And He invites us to join in His work of salvation by being humble ourselves.

Jesus said, "Whoever humbles himself like this child, he is the greatest in the kingdom of heaven" (Mt 18:4) and "Whoever exalts himself will be humbled, and whoever humbles himself will be exalted" (Mt 23:12). Saint James continued this theme and explained that humbling oneself was the key to a relationship with God. Quoting from the Old Testament, he wrote: "God opposes the proud, but gives grace to the humble" (Jas 4:6; Prov 3:34). He therefore exhorted Christians: "Humble yourselves before the Lord and he will exalt you" (4:10). Saint Peter also quoted from the Old Testament when he wrote: "Clothe yourselves, all of you, with humility toward one another, for 'God opposes the proud, but gives grace to the humble.' Humble yourselves therefore under the mighty hand of God, that in due time he may exalt you" (1 Pt 5:5–6).

People of faith are not immune to pride. In fact, they are vul-nerable to the spiritual pride that can distort the good they do. "Beware of practicing your piety before men in order to be seen by them," Jesus warned. "Thus, when you give alms, sound no trum-pet before you, as the hypocrites do in the synagogues and in the streets, that they may be praised by men. Truly, I say to you, they have their reward. But when you give alms, do not let your left hand know what your right hand is doing, so that your alms may be in secret; and your Father who sees in secret will reward you" (Mt 6:1–4). Humility counteracts pride and purifies our motives. It helps us to be grateful for our gifts, to give God the credit for them, and to share them with others as God intends.

Humility also counteracts the various forms of false humility. The first form of false humility, which describes what most people mean by this term, is bragging about being humble in order to impress people with how humble you are. This is a form of pride, and it is usually done in order to exercise control over others. Another kind of false humility is the refusal to recognize your own dignity as a beloved son or daughter of the Father and the gifts and abilities He has given you to share with others. This is pride when it results from comparing ourselves to others and being sad that our talents are not as good as theirs. Finally, there is the false humility that stems from misunderstanding what humility is. Many Christians, in the name of trying to be humble, hide their talents under a bushel basket and don't share them. They think that sharing them is prideful. They also think that developing them and perhaps becoming better at them than some other people is likewise prideful. Nothing could be further from the truth! You see, we give glory to God when we acknowledge the gifts He has given us, develop them, and use them as He intends.

Humility and the Saints

Over and over the saints have told us that humility is the foundation of the spiritual life. It is also the foundation of the happy life. Humility helps us to place ourselves and this world into proper perspective by reminding us that we are creatures of God, and therefore dependent on Him. Humility also reminds us of our dignity, which is the result of our being created in God's image and likeness and being called by God to do great things in imitation of Him and in service to others. Therefore, humility also reminds us of the importance of developing our talents, so that we can fulfill our calling. And it counteracts the constant temptation to pride and false humility.

Saint John Chrysostom said that "humility is the mother, root, nurse, foundation and center of all other virtues."[2] It makes sense that before we would seek to develop virtues we would first need to acknowledge that we lacked them. Many saints have echoed this truth. Saint Bernard of Clairvaux said, "Humility is necessary not only for the acquisition of virtues, but even salvation. For the gate of Heaven, as Christ Himself testifies, is so narrow that it admits only little ones."[3]

Thomas à Kempis, author of the spiritual classic *The Imitation of Christ*, told us how to obtain humility: "Here is one of the best means to acquire humility: fix well in mind this maxim: One is as much as he is in the sight of God, and no more."[4] To put this into practice, think for a moment of how little you are, how often you fail, how often you go astray, how insignificant you are compared to the vastness of the universe or the mystery of God. Now think of how big you are as a beloved son or daughter of the Father, created in His image and likeness, offered a share in His very life, and called to do great things in His service in order to share in His glory. Saint Teresa of Avila, author of the spiritual classic *Interior Castle*, wrote more about humility than anything else.[5] Her insights can be summarized in a quote often attributed to her: "Humility is the courage to live in the truth of who you are." Humility is living in the truth about our smallness and our greatness. Accepting both things about ourselves provides relief regarding our weaknesses and ambition to do better.

During His fast in the wilderness, Jesus overcame the temptations of the devil with the humility of a man who knows He is a son of God (see Mt 4:1–11). With each temptation, He chose obedience to the Father's will instead of heeding the devil's voice to satisfy or to glorify Himself. And the devil left Him. Saint Vincent de Paul explained, "The most powerful weapon to conquer the Devil is humility, for as the Devil does not know at all how to employ it, neither does he know how to defend himself from it."[6] To say that humility is important to a happy and holy life would be an understatement. It is essential.

All of the saints were humble. They lived in the truth of who they were created to be. Mark Mendes, in his booklet *How to Be Somebody*, provides twelve practices given by the saints for growing in humility:

1. Think little of yourself.
2. Do not desire or seek honor or esteem.
3. Accept with patience insults from others.
4. Do not exult in the praise received from others.
5. Remember your sinfulness.
6. Keep your eyes on your own faults, not those of others.
7. Refrain from speaking about yourself.
8. Avoid stubbornness unless the matter deals with truth.
9. Avoid all envy; it is part of pride.
10. Seek and accept advice.
11. Seek and accept correction.
12. Make use of the Sacrament of Reconciliation regularly.[7]

Like the saints, people who practice humility know who they are. They are honest about their strengths and talents, gladly using them to serve others and to glorify God. They are honest about their weaknesses, calling on others when needed and allowing others to help. Although humble people do not exalt themselves, when they are esteemed and honored by others they acknowledge their gifts and strengths, thankfully and genuinely accept the praise, and then give the credit to God.

A Corresponding Beatitude

Jesus said, "Blessed are the meek, for they shall inherit the earth" (Mt 5:5). God gave Adam and Eve a home in a garden. He gave His chosen people a promised land. But God also took away these things when His children became proud and exalted themselves. In order to be in right relationship with God and the created world He gives us as a gift, we must humble ourselves by our obedience to God. We cannot inherit the earth, and take care of it properly, without the virtue of humility. A proud man arrogantly exploits the goods of the earth and other people for his own use, seeing himself as accountable to no one. A humble person, on the other hand, gratefully receives the gifts of God, and with good stewardship uses them and cares for them as God commands. This is the servant "whom his master will set over his household" (Lk 12:42).

Humility and the Temperaments

Choleric

People with a choleric temperament struggle with pride. They are very aware of their strengths and talents, but they often fail to recognize that these are gifts from God. They also tend to criticize others for their weaknesses while downplaying their own. They often underestimate their weaknesses or assume that their strengths will make up for what they lack. Driven by action and the desire for results, cholerics tend not to admit failure, unpreparedness, or weakness and to blame others for the bad outcomes that their shortcomings helped to bring about. They can be prideful about their plan of action and not accept help, support, or critique from others. Cholerics need to understand that they cannot be truly great or pleasing to God without the virtue of humility. They need to commit themselves to acquiring this virtue. And when they do, they are set free, so to speak, to make a true gift of their talents to others and to cooperate with the talents of others in remarkable ways.

Sanguine

Sanguines need to work on humility, not because they are prone to pride, but because they do not possess a lot of self-knowledge. They tend to be guided by their feelings and emotions and often do not reflect deeply enough on their own strengths and weaknesses. Because they are motivated by people and relationships, they may base their identity on these and seek to please others rather than seeking to please God by doing His will. Sanguines need to grow in self-knowledge and to discover how God wants them to use their gifts to serve Him.

Melancholic and Phlegmatic

Melancholics and phlegmatics are nearly polar opposites of each other when it comes to humility. The phlegmatic struggles with self-knowledge but excels at service to others. The melancholic possesses lots of self-knowledge but struggles to serve others. The phlegmatic temperament needs to work at not diminishing or understating his talents and strengths, which is a kind of false humility discussed above. The melancholic is usually keenly aware of both his strengths and weaknesses because he tends to be introspective. However, too much introspection can lead to self-absorption and a reluctance to make the effort to act when one should. The virtue of humility is needed both to know oneself and to obey God's will.

Associated Virtues

The virtue of humility is assisted and practiced more readily when accompanied by these other virtues.

- ○ *Awareness/Mindfulness* is knowing your strengths and weaknesses and reading a situation correctly.
- ○ *Trust* is believing that God has been generous in His gifts to you and will provide what you need to do His will.
- ○ *Gratitude* is giving thanks for all that you have.

Associated Vices

A lack of humility can manifest itself in many ways, and we must be careful of the following vices in order to grow in this virtue:

- • Pride—thinking too highly of yourself. Thinking you are capable of a task without preparing for it or asking others for help. *Steals the joy of being honest about weakness and relying on others.*
- • False Humility—denying your abilities because of pretense, low self-esteem, or false notions of humility. *Steals the joy of contributing your gifts in service of God and others.*

- Laziness—failing to give the situation the attention and the effort it deserves. *Steals the joy of being in right relationship with others and growing in trust and friendship.*
- Vanity—admiring yourself too much, especially your physical appearance. *Steals the joy being able to see past appearances.*

Practical Ways to Grow

That's the textbook stuff, but let's talk for a moment about humility in action, and what it takes to develop this virtue at work, at home, and in life. To have humility, a person needs to do four things:

1. Recognize your own dignity as a beloved son or daughter of the Father created in His image.
2. Acknowledge your strengths and weaknesses.
3. Seek to please the Lord above everything else.
4. Be willing to use your gifts to glorify God and to serve others and to let others do the same.

Growing in humility is a long process. Right when you think you have mastered humility, you will learn that it was your pride that thought so. Take courage and don't be afraid of how humility will change your perspective and your life. Admitting that we are not perfect, that we are broken, is important, but so too is it important to admit that we have gifts and talents and abilities that we can use to glorify God in the service of ourselves and others.

Practice humility by growing in self-awareness. Bring your need to grow in this virtue to prayer. The Lord seems to answer prayers for patience and humility quicker than any other. Pray for humility, and the Lord will give you lots of opportunities to be humbled. Ask God to show you the gifts he wants you to use to glorify Him and to serve others. Then use those gifts; do not hide them! Ask Him to show you which gifts He wants you to develop. Then develop those gifts! If you need help from others, practice humility by asking for it.

Remember that humility, like all the virtues, comes from repeatedly practicing this virtue, while cooperating with God's grace. By practicing humility daily, you will build up this important spiritual muscle, and you will more easily reject pride and find peace in trusting in God's providence. You will be freer to make a gift of yourself to others and to let them contribute their gifts to you.

Litany of Humility

Rafael Cardinal Merry del Val (1865–1930), secretary to Pope Pius X, wrote the classic Litany of Humility. Below is a modified and updated version by Father Joseph Martin Hagan, O.P., first published in Dominicana (February 20, 2017). We offer it with the author's permission and suggest that this become a frequent part of your prayer life. If you struggle with humility, pray it daily and trust that God will give you many opportunities to practice this essential virtue.

O Jesus, meek and humble of heart, teach me.

From all pride and its effects, *deliver me, Jesus.*
From coveting greatness for its own sake or to excess, *etc.*
From contempt of You and Your law,
From a puffed-up self-image,
From claiming to be a self-made man,
From ingratitude for Your gifts,
From thinking that I have earned Your gifts by my effort
    alone,
From boasting of having what I do not have,
From excusing my faults while judging others,
From wishing to be the sole possessor of the skills I have,
From setting myself before others,
From all vainglory, *deliver me, Jesus.*
From craving praise for its own sake, *etc.*
From looking for flattery,
From withholding glory from You,
From showing off to the harm of my neighbor,
From presumption and false self-confidence,
From boastfulness,
From hypocrisy,
From the excessive need to be fashionable,

From obstinacy and contention,
From disobedience,
From all false humility, *deliver me, Jesus.*
From forfeiting my dignity as a child of God, *etc.*
From burying the talents that You gave me,
From an unreasonable fear of failure,
From avoiding my true vocation,
From despair at my weakness,

In the ways of humility, *teach me, Jesus.*
To know my limits and my strengths, *etc.*
To acknowledge the depravity of my past sins,
To acclaim You as the author of all the good I do,
To put my confidence in You,
To be subject to You and Your Church,
To be subject to others for Your sake,
To revere Your presence in others,
To rejoice in Your gifts in others, even the gifts unseen,

To do great things by Your help and for Your glory,
   strengthen me, Jesus.
To seek greatness in heavenly things and lasting virtue, *etc.*
To do my best even when unnoticed,
To put my share of Your gifts at Your service,
To be neither puffed up by honor nor downcast by shame,
To do penance for my sins and those of others,
Above all, to strive to love You with all my being,
And to love my neighbor as myself,
In Your name, I pray. Amen.

13

Obedience

"He who gives heed to the word will prosper, and happy is he who trusts in the LORD."

—Proverbs 16:20

The virtue of obedience is the habit of doing what is asked or required of us and of responding promptly to the will of God. With all the focus on autonomy, freedom, and individualism in our society, we often undervalue or even scorn obedience. We tend not to aspire to this virtue; instead, we tend to lionize rebels. Consequently, obedience to authority figures in our country is at an all-time low. We frequently hear media reports of disrespect, and sometimes even violence, toward police officers, teachers, and parents.

True Obedience

Apart from the fact that, thanks to the Fall, we all have a rebellious streak, one reason obedience is a neglected virtue is that many people do not understand what it really is. Obedience is often seen as being about conforming to the arbitrary wills of those above us rather than about doing what is right and good for the benefit of all.

Every organization, every common effort, requires a certain amount of order and hierarchy. Practically nothing worth doing can be done without a chain of command, however flawed the people in that chain are sure to be. You couldn't board a plane and expect to arrive at your destination if there were not layers of authority figures committed to your doing that—from air traffic control, to the captain of the plane, to the flight crew. When the captain sees turbulence ahead and commands that you fasten your seatbelt, it would be stupid to disobey.

The word *obedience* comes from a Latin word meaning "to listen to". Obedience requires paying attention and docility, an ability to be taught or led, coupled with a trusting openness to those in charge. I can follow the instructions of my boss begrudgingly, complaining about it to my colleagues and undermining the authority of my superior, but this, as you can guess, is not true obedience. This is merely following instructions, perhaps only out of fear of losing my job. True obedience is not driven by fear or blind obligation; it is driven by giving those in authority the benefit of the doubt that they seek to serve the common good and then listening to them with respect. Are there times when we are called upon to resist those in authority? Yes, but in such cases we must be listening to a higher authority— God Himself.

While true obedience involves promptness, Jesus told a parable that shows that the main thing is doing the right thing. "A man had two sons; and he went to the first and said, 'Son, go and work in the vineyard today.' And he answered, 'I will not'; but afterward he repented and went. And he went to the second and said the same; and he answered, 'I go, sir,' but did not go. Which of the two did the will of his father?" (Mt 21:28–31). The crowd responded correctly, saying that the first son obeyed his father by ultimately doing what his father asked him to do. Those who have developed the virtue of obedience gladly do what others in proper authority ask, when it is the right thing to do, and do so promptly and with integrity. And they complete the task to the best of their ability.

Obedience is a necessary virtue because we must trust others and align our wills with theirs in order to accomplish goals that we could not or would not want to accomplish on our own. In life, there are three fundamental relationships, which we have discussed throughout this book, that require obedience: with God, with others, and with creation. Let us look at what obedience looks like within the context of these relationships.

Obedience to God

First and foremost, we must be obedient to God because He created us, loves us, and wills what is best for us. And He has revealed to us how to obey Him, generally through the Ten Commandments, the main teachings of Christ (as found in the Sermon on the Mount, see Mt 5–7), and by His modeling for us what true obedience to the Father looks like. God also reveals to each of us more specifically what He has in mind for us if we but listen to His voice. Our obedience to God is central to our being happy, because He knows who we are and what we need better than we do. Obedience to Him is not a sign of weakness, but of true wisdom and strength born from a listening and teachable spirit.

Once there was a father who asked his son to build him a home. The son was a skilled carpenter, and the father gave him the plan and asked that he spare no expense in carrying it out. The son, however, cut corners and costs wherever he could. He built a beautiful home, but the joints were loose, the walls were not properly finished, and the materials, including the fixtures, were of poor quality. His father never stopped by the house while it was being built, and he paid all the bills without questions. When the house was finished, the father came over and, without even setting foot inside, gave his son a hug and the keys and said, "You weren't building this home for me; you were building it for you. It is yours."

When God asks us to do things, according to His specifications, He is asking on our behalf. He doesn't need us to do things for Him; we need to do what He asks for our own good. And when we don't, we are the ones who suffer the consequences of our disobedience or laziness. God invites us to share in His work of creation and salvation because this is what brings us happiness. And being obedient to Him is the key to our participation in His life.

Obedience to Others

In addition to His commandments, God reveals His will for us through our relationships and circumstances in life. Thus, when we obey the directives of those in authority over us, provided they are not asking us to sin, we are obeying God. When we are young, the authorities are our parents and those who guide us in their place, such as teachers. When we are adults, they are those who maintain civil and religious order: legislatures, police, judges, bishops, and so on.

There is another kind of obedience to God that we discover in our relationships with others, the obedience of love. The reciprocal giving of oneself in friendship, in family life, and in community living necessarily requires this kind of obedience—that is, gladly listening to and responding to the needs of the other. True obedience in these contexts does not come from fear or even a sense of fairness, but from the desire to serve the good of the other.

In every human community the reciprocal nature of obedience is present, and we see this most clearly in the family, where, for example, my child is obedient to my request to make his bed, and I am obedient to his needs for food, shelter, education, and a loving environment. This kind of obedience often requires that I place the needs of others before my own, as when my wife had a hard day and I forego watching a game in order to be present to her. Sometimes Jesus asks us to respond to the needs of those outside our ordinary relationships, where no apparent reciprocity exists, as He did with the Parable of the Good Samaritan, who rescued and cared for a total stranger as if he were his own flesh and blood. When we heed the voice of conscience in a situation like this, that too is obeying God.

The mutual understanding and agreements between employers and employees also extend reciprocal rights and obligations. The employer has the right to make demands of his employees, who have the obligation to work diligently and to follow the instructions of their superiors. The employees also have rights—to their pay and to their time off to fulfill other responsibilities. In order to be truly human, the workplace should be a place where we can hear and respond to the calling to love like the Good Samaritan—as when a single employee offers to work on a holiday so that someone with a family can have the day off, or when an employer finishes the work of a sick employee, and so on.

Obedience in relationships is more than just doing what I am told, it is about gladly listening and responding to the needs of others out of a desire to serve them and make a gift of myself. The virtue of obedience, born out of love for the other, looks less like following orders and more like listening to God's command to love others as ourselves.

Obedience to Creation

The third fundamental relationship is with the created world. We are told that nature is our first teacher. We learn much from interacting with our environment, and we learn at a young age that we must be obedient to it. We mustn't touch things that are hot, because they will burn us. We mustn't riskily climb too high, lest gravity bring us down. And so on. Our relationship with nature is such that when we listen and respond to it, by exercising proper dominion, nature is also obedient to us. When we learn how nature works, we can bring about its abundance. This is true both in cultivating food and in developing technologies.

When we make unreasonable demands of nature or fail to care for it properly, we abuse it to our own detriment. When we degrade the air we breathe, the water we drink, and the soil we need to raise crops, we poison ourselves. When we treat animals cruelly, we diminish our own dignity. Wendell Berry, the great agricultural essayist and poet, has spent a lifetime calling people back into proper relationship with the land. He wrote, "The ecological teaching of the Bible is simply inescapable: God made the world because He wanted it made. He thinks the world is good, and He loves it. It is His world; He has never relinquished title to it. And He has never revoked the conditions, bearing on His gift to us of the use of it, that oblige us to take excellent care of it."[1] Because of the Fall, our relationship with creation is strained, but we must learn to respect it, trusting that God has made everything we need to care for ourselves. As the prophet Isaiah said, "If you are willing and obedient, you shall eat the good of the land" (Is 1:19).

Unfortunately, also because of the Fall, we tend to enjoy being in command, but tend to resist the commands of our superiors. It is easy to tell others what to do, and to expect a lot from them. Yet, it is hard to respect and to obey others. This is why developing the virtue of obedience is so important. First we need to listen and to respond to God—His word and His will for our life. And that involves listening and responding to the people He has placed in our lives—being docile to what authority figures say and being responsive to the needs of others. And second, we need to learn how to be in right relationship with creation, so that it in turn will bless us with fruitfulness for generations to come.

Obedience in Scripture

The Scriptures place obedience at the center of the drama of salvation. We can either be obedient to God or, in our pride, reject Him. As Pope Benedict said, "At the heart of all temptations ... is the act of pushing God aside because we perceive him as secondary."[2] The story of the Fall in Genesis is about disobedience, while the Old Testament covenant was about obedience. We can either be obedient and faithful to the covenant God offers us, and receive its many blessings, or reject His covenant and suffer the consequences. "And because you listen to these ordinances, and keep and do them, the LORD your God will keep with you the covenant and the merciful love which he swore to your fathers to keep" (Deut 7:12).

Before the Israelites entered the promised land, the Lord reminded them: "I have set before you life and death, blessing and curse; therefore choose life, that you and your descendants may live, loving the LORD your God, obeying his voice, and clinging to him; for that means life to you and length of days" (Deut 30:19–20). The exhortation is simple: obey and have life, or disobey and be left to your own devices.

The New Testament reveals how God's plan to save us comes through the obedience of Jesus Christ, who submits Himself to the will of the Father. "I have come down from heaven, not to do my own will, but the will of him who sent me" (Jn 6:38). "For as by one man's disobedience many were made sinners, so by one man's obedience many will be made righteous" (Rom 5:19). Jesus, the obedient Son, gains for us the reward of eternal life, and He heals the wound and division, in us and in creation, caused by sin. Even the seas and the wind obey Jesus (see Mt 8:27), who calls people to obey God, not just by keeping His commandments, but by living in right relationship with God, each other, and creation.

There are serious and eternal consequences for refusing to obey God, but there also are tremendous rewards for repenting of our rebellion and obeying Him. "He who believes in the Son has eternal life; he who does not obey the Son shall not see life" (Jn 3:36). Obedience is also deeply practical. "Children, obey your parents in the Lord, for this is right. 'Honor your father and mother' (this is the first commandment with a promise), 'that it may be well with you and that you may live long on the earth'" (Eph 6:1–3). The fact is, when we refuse to obey God, we are actually obeying the temptation to sin, which leads to misery. "Do you not know that if you yield yourselves to any one as obedient slaves, you are slaves of the one whom you obey, either of sin, which leads to death, or of obedience, which leads to righteousness?" (Rom 6:16). The drama of good and evil, of happiness and misery is played out in the simple question: "Whom will you obey, God or something else?"

Obedience and the Saints

The saints are full of wisdom regarding the virtue of obedience. They persevered in obedience to God's will, and they provide for us shining examples of what it looks like to obey God and others.

Saint Vincent de Paul said that all of creation is called to be obedient to God. "All the good of creatures consists in the fulfillment of the Divine Will. And this is never better attained than by the practice of obedience, in which is found the annihilation of self-love and the true liberty of sons of God. This is the reason why souls truly good, experience such great joy and sweetness in obedience."[3]

Echoing Scripture, the saints pointed out the centrality of obedience in a life pleasing to God. The Lord said through the prophet Samuel, "Behold, to obey is better than sacrifice" (1 Sam 15:22), and He told Saint Faustina, "My daughter, know that you give Me greater glory by a single act of obedience than by long prayers and mortifications."[4] Saint Frances de Sales said, "Many have been Saints without meditation, but without obedience, no one!"[5] While there are many ways to pray, and many ways to grow in holiness, there is only one way to be obedient, which is to listen to God and to do His will.

Saint Ignatius of Loyola explained the three elements of obedience. "That obedience may be complete, it must exist in three things: in execution, by doing promptly, cheerfully, and exactly whatever the Superior orders; in will, by willing nothing but what the Superior wills; in judgment, by being of the same opinion as the Superior."[6] Ignatius had been a soldier, and he understood that a person's strength comes from being obedient. Saint Teresa of Avila beautifully described this paradox when she wrote, "I often thought my constitution would never endure the work I had to do, (but) the Lord said to me: 'Daughter, obedience gives strength.'"[7]

When Ryan was a teenager, his mother told him that whenever his friends were doing something wrong, he should leave after saying, "I do not want to get in trouble with my Mom." She said, "Use obeying me as an excuse to do good, until you are able to do it on your own." That obedience actually gave Ryan the courage and the freedom to do what he knew was right.

Like the saints, a person who practices the virtue of obedience listens and gladly responds to the promptings of God and the requests of others. Obedient people are not weak, rather they have learned the truth that we are meant to serve God and serve others. We are made freer by being obedient to God's word and His will, instead of to our own self-will, which ultimately leads to unhappiness.

A Corresponding Beatitude

Jesus calls us to obedience in His teaching and most dramatically through the example of His life. He is the perfectly obedient Son, who revealed to us the compassionate love of the Father and the power of the Holy Spirit. His first beatitude is "Blessed are the poor in spirit, for theirs is the kingdom of Heaven" (Mt 5:3). Those who are poor in spirit are docile to God, and that is why they are capable of living in the kingdom of heaven.

The citizens of God's kingdom aren't proud, boastful, and assertive. They aren't self-righteous either, even though that is the caricature that many people have of faithful Christians. Father Raniero Cantalamessa, O.F.M. Cap., who has served as a preacher to the Papal Household, explained that being poor in spirit "banishes animosity and judgment, substituting instead a reciprocal esteem for, and joy in, the good that God accomplishes through others".[8] The kingdom of heaven is for those who know that they and everyone else are dependent on God and His mercy.

Typically, those who know most keenly that they need God are those lacking in material wealth. They appreciate the little they have and receive it gratefully as a gift from the Lord. The Aramaic word that Christ likely used for "the poor" refers to those who are bowed down, meaning oppressed or crushed by the challenges of this world. It is those who, though brought low, keep their eyes on the Lord, trusting in Him as the provider of all good gifts.

Study after study has shown that that those who have less material wealth are actually happier, more joyful, and more generous with the little they have than those who have more. They appreciate the goods of this world, but they know that this world will never be enough to fulfill the desires of their hearts, which long for the Lord. The poor in spirit begin to live in God's kingdom while still here on earth because the Lord, not their own ego and ambition, is already their all in all. They are not only docile and humble, but also obedient to God's will, because they gladly submit their own nothingness to Him.

Obedience and the Temperaments

Choleric

People with a choleric temperament are motivated by action. They are doers and love to respond to a challenge. In both the family and the workplace, cholerics can rise to the challenge of a particular task with great energy, and they can willingly obey a mission entrusted to them. However, since they are prone to arrogance and acting quickly, they may not listen well. As a result, they may not be obedient. They can be heedless of instructions, thinking that they already know what to do or can figure it out on their own.

To develop the virtue of obedience, the choleric temperament needs to listen carefully to both the instructions and the goals of their superiors. They must fight the proud assumption that they know what to do and ask for help, correction, and guidance along the way.

Sanguine

The sanguine temperament struggles with the perseverance needed to be obedient until the end. Because they are natural people pleasers, sanguines have no trouble listening to others, but they can lack judgment about prioritizing which others they actually need to obey. They must cultivate the virtue of obedience by being obedient to God first, family second, central commitments third, and other things fourth.

Phlegmatic

The phlegmatic temperament does not often struggle with developing obedience. Phlegmatics are peace-makers and make excellent diplomats, able to negotiate complex situations with grace and poise. They both listen to and willingly fulfill the requests of others. Sometimes phlegmatics struggle with initiating activity, which can appear as being disobedient. Phlegmatics need to ask questions in order to understand the expectations of others. They are rule-followers and can be obedient to the commandments of God with the right spirit if they let those commands live in their heart, not just their head. They need to spend time in prayer in order to hear with confidence the promptings of God in their lives.

Melancholic

The melancholic temperament is loyal and deep. Motivated by ideas, melancholics can be fiercely obedient to their convictions. They listen well, and they tend to be loyal to those they care about. However, they are prone to exaggerating problems, and sometimes they lack obedience simply from wanting more assurance than the situation can provide. They need to have courage in the form of audacity to be obedient to valid orders that may be difficult or unclear.

Associated Virtues

The virtue of obedience is assisted and practiced more readily when accompanied by these other virtues.

- ◦ *Acceptance* is accepting what you can and cannot control.
- ◦ *Docility* is the willingness to be flexible and ready to say yes to God's plan as revealed by the promptings of the Holy Spirit.
- ◦ *Openness* is not letting changing conditions steal your joy.

Associated Vices

A lack of obedience can manifest itself in many ways, and we must be careful of these vices in order to grow in obedience.

- Pride—thinking too highly of yourself. Thinking you are capable of a task without preparation or help from others. *Steals the joy of being honest about weakness and relying on others.*
- Laziness—failing to give the situation the attention and the effort it deserves. *Steals the joy of being in right relationships with others and of growing in trust and friendship.*

Practical Ways to Grow

So, you've been reading the textbook stuff, but let us talk for a moment about real obedience in action, and what it takes to develop this virtue at work, at home, and in life. To have obedience, a person needs to do three things:

1. Obey God and others with cheerfulness and courage.
2. Be willing to submit your will to another's, in the pursuit of things that are good and just.
3. Listen and promptly do the thing requested to the best of your ability.

Growing in obedience takes a lot of trust, docility, and a real desire to serve the good of others. When we learn to be obedient in small things, greater demands of obedience become easier. Think of all the areas of your life in which you are called to be obedient. Let us start small. Are you being obedient to the needs of your body? Are you eating well? Are you exercising? Are you getting enough sleep? Are you waking up on time?

Here are a few more reflective questions. Are you spending within your means? Are you obedient to a budget that is in line with your income and expenses? What about completing your jobs or daily tasks? Are you doing your work to the best of your ability? Are you responsive to the demands made on you by your superiors? Do you do your tasks with gratitude and cheerfulness? Do you actively listen to those whose job it is to give you instructions? Do you listen to those who need your help?

Now, let us get a little more serious, and talk about your *mission*. Are you discerning and responding to what your mission in life is? Are you being obedient to your mission in life? Are you practicing and cultivating your talents? Are you learning and studying the things you need to know in order to complete your mission in life?

Now, let us talk about your *vocation*. If you are married, are you obedient and submissive to your spouse? Are you being faithful to your vows? Are you actively listening and responding to the needs of your family? If you are unmarried, are you keeping your heart chaste and free? Are you developing your personal interests and forming habits that are healthy for relationships? Are you faithful and good to your friends and colleagues?

Finally, let us talk about being *obedient to God*. First, it is worth mentioning that being obedient to God implies and demands that we are obedient in the other areas just discussed. Are you making time daily to pray and to listen to God? Are you following the Ten Commandments and the Precepts of the Church? Do you worship God on Sunday by going to Mass and avoiding unnecessary work? Have you brought major life decisions to the Lord and followed His will? Are you living the beatitudes?

By practicing obedience daily, you will build up this important spiritual muscle and more easily reject pride. You will find peace in humbly submitting yourself to the service of God and others.

14

Generosity

"Give to the Most High as he has given, and as generously as your hand has found."

—Sirach 35:10

The virtue of generosity is the habit of giving abundantly in the service of others. Generous people all share something in common: they care more about people than material things. And they find joy in giving, helping, and contributing to the well-being of others. Some people are so generous that they give not only from their surplus but also from what they need for themselves, in defiance of their instincts for self-preservation. Jesus praised the Jewish widow who "out of her poverty" gave the Temple "all the living that she had" (Lk 21:14). It doesn't make a lot of sense until we understand what Jesus does: "Give, and it will be given to you; good measure, pressed down, shaken together, running over, will be put into your lap. For the measure you give will be the measure you get back" (Lk 6:38).

One of the highest compliments you can receive is the words: "That was very generous of you." A generous act is a gift of oneself—whether it be one's time, talent, or treasure—and it is often gratefully acknowledged by others. But we shouldn't give in order to be thanked and praised or because we have so much extra (though many of us do). Rather, we should give because we are made in the image and likeness of God, who pours Himself out for us so that we can be like Him by pouring ourselves out for others. The fact is, we need to give in order to be the man or the woman God has created us to be. As Billy Graham explained, "God has given us two hands, one to receive with and the other to give with. We are not cisterns made for hoarding; we are channels made for sharing."[1]

Most people would probably agree that they would be better people, and the world around them a better place, if they would stretch themselves a little to be more generous. They know that they could forego that cup of overpriced coffee and have more money to give to a worthy charity. They could cut back their screen time and have more time to play with their children, visit a relative in a nursing home, or call a lonely person on the phone. If we know these things yet find ourselves reluctant to do them, that means we need to grow in the virtue of generosity.

Christian Generosity

The first Christians were the most generous people the world had ever seen. In the early days of the Church, Christians shared everything they had with one another and especially with the poor (see Acts 2:44–47). Pagans were amazed at the generosity of Christians, saying "See how they love!"[2] It was just as Jesus had foretold, "By this all men will know that you are my disciples, if you have love for one another" (Jn 13:35). Because of the generous love of the first Christians, the Church grew exponentially.

In all times and places Christians are called to be generous, "for this is the message which you have heard from the beginning, that we should love one another" (1 Jn 3:11). The first reason Christians are generous is the Lord's own example. "By this we know love, that he laid down his life for us; and we ought to lay down our lives for the brethren" (1 Jn 3:16). Second, we believe that everything we have is a gift from God, our loving Father, and is meant to be shared with others. "Every good endowment and every perfect gift is from above, coming down from the Father" (Jas 1:17). Third, we trust that God will provide for us. "His divine power has granted to us all things that pertain to life and godliness" (2 Pt 1:3). And finally, we know that the material world is good but that possessing and consuming things cannot make us truly happy. "Is not life more than food, and the body more than clothing?" (Mt 6:25).

Jesus and the first Christians were Jews, who knew well God's command to care for widows and their fatherless children. Among the first official works of mercy carried out by the early Church was the distribution of food to widows (see Acts 6:1–3). As Saint James wrote, "Religion that is pure and undefiled before God and the Father is this: to visit orphans and widows in their affliction, and to keep oneself unstained from the world" (Jas 1:27).

The Catholic Church has been caring for the poor, the widowed, the orphaned, and the sick from the beginning. It is probably safe to say that she has performed more works of mercy than any other institution in human history. When Tom first researched the charitable work of the Church for the script of *Epic*—a Catholics Come Home Evangomercial that continues to air all over the world—he was amazed at the sheer volume of charitable work the Church does every year. He discovered that the Church is the largest charitable organization on the planet.[3] We can take authentic pride in all the Church has done, and continues to do, in the name of Christ, so long as we participate in this work through our generous contributions of time, talent, and treasure.

The Power of a Good Example

A priest celebrating the fiftieth anniversary of his ordination told a story of when he was a young seminarian on a mission trip. He was hosted by a poor, elderly couple who lived in a small one-bedroom house with no running water. They offered to sleep on the couch so that he could have their bedroom. They patiently taught him how to pronounce the difficult words in their native language. And they fed him from their meager supply of food. At mealtime, their home was full of neighborhood children and those poorer than they were who knew they could find something to eat at their generous table. "Their hearts were so open," the priest said, "open to the very real possibility that God might just use their small offering as part of His great plan in this world." He was so struck by their joy, he added. "They were happiest when they were giving of themselves. I thought to myself, back then: I want to have an open and generous heart like they have." Anne Frank wrote that "no one has ever become poor by giving."[4] In fact, it seems that giving makes people truly rich.

Chances are we have all benefitted from someone else's generosity and can likely remember how much it warmed our heart and lifted our spirits, renewing our faith not only in God but in our fellow man. The act of generosity probably made a deep impression on us, inspiring us to be generous too. That's what happened to the famous composer Johannes Brahms when an admirer of his music left him one thousand British pounds. He wrote to his friend, "It touches me most deeply and intimately. All exterior honors are nothing in comparison." He added that he would be "taking pleasure in its distribution".[5] See how generosity breeds more generosity?

That is precisely the effect Benjamin Franklin was hoping for when he sent money to a young friend in 1784. He wrote, "I do not pretend to *give* such a sum; I only *lend* it to you.... [W]hen you meet with another honest man in similar distress, you must pay me by lending this sum to him; enjoining him to discharge the debt by a like operation, when he shall be able, and shall meet with such another opportunity. I hope it may thus go through many hands, before it meets with a knave that will stop its progress."[6] We have our contemporary equivalents of this sort of thing. The unofficial record for paying it forward at a drive-thru was set in 2019 at a coffee shop in Saint Petersburg, Florida, where reportedly 378 people paid for the order behind them. That's the power of a good example and the power of generosity, which is the most contagious of virtues.

Generosity in Scripture

Jesus said that at the Last Judgment "the King will say to those at his right hand, 'Come, O blessed of my Father, inherit the kingdom prepared for you from the foundation of the world; for I was hungry and you gave me food, I was thirsty and you gave me drink, I was a stranger and you welcomed me, I was naked and you clothed me, I was sick and you visited me, I was in prison and you came to me.' " Jesus also said that the righteous will ask the King when they did these things for Him, "and the King will answer them, 'Truly, I say to you, as you did it to one of the least of these my brethren, you did it to me' " (Mt 25:34–40). The meaning is clear: God, who has been so generous to us, wants us to be generous to others and to treat them as we would treat Him.

The idea that when we give to the poor, we give to God Himself is also in the Old Testament: "He who is kind to the poor lends to the LORD, and he will repay him for his deed" (Prov 19:17). The Law of Moses is very clear about the generosity God expects of His children. "If there is among you a poor man, one of your brethren, in any of your towns within your land which the LORD your God gives you, you shall not harden your heart or shut your hand against your poor brother" (Deut 15:7). And we find the same command in the New Testament: "If any one has the world's goods and sees his brother in need, yet closes his heart against him, how does God's love abide in him? Little children, let us not love in word or speech but in deed and in truth" (1 Jn 3:17–18).

Greed

While Scripture extols the virtue of generosity, it decries the opposing vice of greed, which is an excessive desire for material possessions. "All day long the wicked covets, but the righteous gives and does not hold back" (Prov 21:26). Jesus warned, "Beware of all covetousness; for a man's life does not consist in the abundance of his possessions" (Lk 12:15). Saint Paul said, "The love of money is the root of all evils; it is through this craving that some have wandered away from the faith and pierced their hearts with many pangs" (1 Tim 6:10). These words are not easy to hear, but we must hear them.

Wealth is not bad; in fact, we can use it to do a great amount of good. But it can be the downfall of a person if he doesn't counter the tendency to greed by making the effort to be generous. Our blessings are not meant for ourselves alone (regardless of how hard we worked for them). God gave them to us so that we would share them with others and participate in His own generosity. Thus the apostles taught: "As for the rich in this world, charge them not to be haughty, nor to set their hopes on uncertain riches but on God who richly furnishes us with everything to enjoy. They are to do good, to be rich in good deeds, liberal and generous, thus laying up for themselves a good foundation for the future, so that they may take hold of the life which is life indeed" (1 Tim 6:17–19).

Greed turns our focus in on ourselves, eats away at our capacity for love, and eventually destroys us. J. R. R. Tolkien's character of Gollum, in *The Lord of the Rings*, is an example of what unchecked greed can do to a person—turn him into a murderous monster. Scrooge, the famous miser from *A Christmas Carol* by Charles Dickens, also illustrates what greed can do—make a man a joyless, loveless loner. No one wants to be Gollum or Scrooge. The solution to preventing *Gollumness* or *Scrooginess* is by growing in and practicing generosity. You could say that generosity inoculates us against the modern-day disease of affluenza, which is accumulating too much stuff.

Generosity and Joy

We are the least happy when we are focused on ourselves. When we give generously, we are thinking of others instead of ourselves, and the result is joy. When Tom was speaking at a conference for West African priests and nuns now serving in America, he was struck by how joyful they all were. He said, "We Americans need more joy in our lives." One Nigerian nun raised her hand and said, "J.O.Y.: Jesus, Others, You—in that order!" Then she added, "You Americans came to evangelize Africa over a century ago, but now we are coming here, to help re-evangelize America!" And they are re-evangelizing us, because their joy, which flows from their generous love for God and others, attracts others to Christ. As Mother Teresa said, "Joy is a net by which we catch souls."[7]

Because generosity causes joy, it is the most contagious of virtues. While greed turns our focus in on ourselves and makes us selfish and unattractive to others, generosity makes us alive and available, which is attractive to others. All of us are attracted to generous people because we all want to be treated as though we matter. And the more generosity we see, the more generous we want to be.

Generosity and the Saints

The saints show us how to make a generous gift of ourselves to God and to others. In *The Hidden Power of Kindness*, Father Lawrence

Lovasik, S.V.D., wrote, "The saints were saints because they were cheerful when it was difficult to be cheerful, patient when it was difficult to be patient, silent when they wanted to speak, and agreeable when they felt an urge to scream. They pushed forward when they wanted to stand still. *Sainthood* is simply another word for self-forgetfulness and generosity."[8]

Saints Benedict and Scholastica taught that generosity can take many forms but always begins in the home or, for them, the monastery. Then generosity extends outward to whomever God might send. The monastic communities they founded are known for their hospitality, which flows from one of the most important Benedictine rules of life: "Let all guests who arrive be received as Christ."[9] In ancient times, hospitality was considered an important mark of a virtuous man, and in the Old Testament we see Abraham hosting three strangers who turned out to be angels. That is why we find in the New Testament: "Do not neglect to show hospitality to strangers, for thereby some have entertained angels unawares" (Heb 13:2).

While being generous begins at home, much of the focus of Christian generosity is on the poor. "If you desire that God should hear your prayers," explained Saint Thomas of Villanova, "hear the voice of the poor . . . especially anticipate the necessities of those ashamed to beg."[10] Saint Basil the Great wrote, "The bread you store up belongs to the hungry; the cloak that lies in your chest belongs to the naked; the gold you have hidden in the ground belongs to the poor."[11] Saint Ambrose, bishop of Milan and mentor to Saint Augustine, told his flock, "The rich man who gives to the poor does not bestow alms but pays a debt."[12] To follow the advice of these saints requires us to go beyond the comfort of home, which is challenging to say the least.

A great example of stretching oneself to serve the poor is Saint Vincent de Paul, who was born to French peasant farmers in 1581. After he became a priest, he was placed in charge of distributing the alms collected at Mass. His visits to the sick, the imprisoned, the dying, and the hungry on the streets of his small town became his central ministry. Soon, other priests, religious sisters, and lay men and women began helping him with visits to those in need. Among these was Saint Louise de Marillac, who, with the help of Saint Vincent, founded the Daughters of Charity, which organized hospitals, orphanages, and workshops for the unemployed. Almost two hundred years later, Blessed Frédéric Ozanam, a Catholic law student in Paris, was challenged by another student to show how he put his faith into action. Ozanam responded by founding the Society of Saint Vincent de Paul to help the poor, as it continues to do in 147 countries today. Through generosity, he became a credible witness of the Gospel.

A Corresponding Beatitude

"Blessed are the merciful," Jesus said, "for they shall obtain mercy" (Mt 5:7). Here, the word *mercy* refers not only to forgiveness but to the generous response one has to the needs of others. Merciful people are, by definition, generous, because they see the needs of others not as burdens, but as opportunities to help and to share. They see serving others not as an imposition, but as a privilege.

There is a clear cause-and-effect relationship between generosity and holiness. The more generous we are, the more we give of ourselves. The more we give of ourselves, the more we depend on God. The more we depend on God, the more we are open to what He offers. The more we are open to what He offers, the more we want what He wants for us and others. The more we want what He wants for us and others, the more open we are to the Holy Spirit living within us and moving within us to align our wills to the will of God. And the more we do that, the more we become who we are meant to be.

Saint Paul said, "The point is this: he who sows sparingly will also reap sparingly, and he who sows bountifully will also reap bountifully" (2 Cor 9:6). This is true not because God is judgmental but because it is the way the universe He made works. Imagine a cup filled up with water; you can't add more water until some of that water has been poured out. We are to be like a spring-fed pond, which gives its water freely and is then refilled. To do this, you need to trust that "God is able to provide you with every blessing in abundance, so that you may always have enough of everything and may provide in abundance for every good work" (2 Cor 9:8).

Think for a moment of how generous God has been to you. He has given you your life, health, family, and friends. Through the contributions of countless other people, God has given you the experiences that have taught you everything you know and the opportunities to use what you have learned. He has provided for your many needs, helped you through many trials, put a balm on your many wounds, and forgiven your many sins. As Jesus would say, "Now go and do likewise" (Lk 10:37).

Generosity and the Temperaments

Choleric

People with a choleric temperament are motivated by action. They are natural doers and love to respond to a challenge. They are capable of great generosity but need to respond prudently to the needs of others. Because they are action oriented, they can sometimes seek to fix the problem, or assert themselves, without really listening to the needs of those they want to serve. Cholerics might assume they know the solution, or they may act before thinking through the ramifications of their action. Humbly discerning how they can helpfully make a gift of themselves is important for cholerics seeking to grow in generosity.

Sanguine

Sanguines love people and are motivated by relationships. Being generous with time, talent, and treasure is not difficult for the sanguine. However, being present over the long haul and entering into the challenges faced by those they want to serve can be a struggle. Sanguines like to feel good, and they tend to want simple and quick solutions. They often struggle with patience. Because being generous requires more than just a one-time act, they need to grow in their ability to persevere. They also need to develop the virtue of generosity by striving to be in solidarity with those they seek to serve.

Phlegmatic

People with a phlegmatic temperament are motivated by peace. They have a keen sense of justice and are naturally drawn toward healing and restoring the brokenness around them. Phlegmatics can be very generous but may be moved more by calculations than by the heart. This is not necessarily a bad thing, but being generous to others is not a mathematical equation; it is ultimately a gift and requires risk. Phlegmatics need to stretch themselves to be generous not just because it is the right thing to do, but because they have heartfelt compassion for the person who needs help.

Melancholic

People with the melancholic temperament are motivated by ideas. They tend to be deep and to have rich interior lives. They can empathize with others and can often intuit what the other person needs. However, they often feel unqualified or unable to help. They may struggle with doing anything at all because they are worried about doing the wrong thing. The melancholic temperament needs to practice being generous in small ways and to grow in confidence that even small acts of generosity can make a big difference.

Associated Virtues

The virtue of generosity is assisted and practiced more readily when accompanied by these other virtues.

- *Mercy* is responding compassionately to someone in need.
- *Forgiveness* is pardoning others for what they have done wrong.
- *Courtesy* is showing respect for others by treating them politely.
- *Charity* is loving God and others through a gift of yourself.
- *Selflessness* is forgetting about yourself in service of another.
- *Hospitality* is warmly receiving and caring for guests and visitors.
- *Gratitude* is giving thanks for all that you have, which is all from God.

Associated Vices

A lack of generosity can manifest itself in many ways, and we must be careful of these vices if we lack generosity.

- Greed—grasping material possessions beyond what you need and refusing to share them. *Steals the joy of serving others and sharing one's blessings.*

- Apathy—not caring about the well-being of other people. *Steals the joy of loving others and serving their needs.*
- Envy—resenting the possessions and the successes of others. *Steals the joy of sharing in someone else's blessings.*
- Laziness—failing to give the situation the attention and the effort it deserves. *Steals your ability to use your particular gifts to serve others.*

Practical Ways to Grow

That's the textbook stuff, but let us talk for a moment about generosity in action and what it takes to develop this virtue at work, at home, and in life. To have generosity, you need four things:

1. Recognition that everything you have is a gift from God
2. Gratitude for God's gifts and a desire to share them with others
3. Trust in God and reliance on His providence
4. Desire to sacrifice for others

Consider for a moment that everything all the Christian churches do throughout the world is done with the typical Christian giving on average less than 2 percent of his income. Imagine what could happen if every Christian gave the tithe, which means 10 percent, that God asks for in the Bible. Imagine if people of great means gave even more than that!

While filming a video about stewardship, Tom learned about the legendary generosity of Saints Anne and Joachim, the parents of Mary and the grandparents of Jesus. They were wealthy and devout and gave one-third of their income to the poor, one-third to the Temple, and lived off the remaining third. We can only marvel at this incredibly generous couple who gave away two-thirds of their income. And look at the fruit in their lives that came from this generosity: the Blessed Mother as their daughter, and Jesus as their grandson! Imagine the blessings that would come if we dug a little deeper to be more generous. For added inspiration here are two stories about bold, but not reckless, charity.

After they became empty-nesters, a successful doctor and his wife, who was a special education teacher at the local high school, wondered what they should do with their large home, which was way too big for just the two of them. They made all the conventional considerations about downsizing and were leaning in that direction. However, their house was paid for, and they felt they needed to do something bold in thanksgiving to God for the life they had lived in that lovely, debt-free home.

After they prayed and asked God to show them what they ought to do, they received a phone call from a dear family friend who fostered children. She said that one of the children she fostered had special needs and was going to undergo surgery in a few weeks. Would the good doctor and his lovely wife be willing to care for the child after the operation? she asked. Taking this as a sign, the couple went through the process of becoming foster parents, and a few weeks later they made arrangements to welcome young Anna into their home. This generous act led them down a beautiful and merciful road they had never imagined. Given both their medical and special education backgrounds, they ended up fostering more children. To prove that God was not without a sense of humor, they not only didn't downsize but added on a large addition to care for even more kids!

Here is a second example. An unmarried schoolteacher saved her money for ten years to purchase her dream home. She didn't eat out, and her vacations consisted of helping at her aunt and uncle's peach farm in Georgia. After she had saved enough for a down payment, she began looking for a cute little house to buy. One day at church, she saw just what she wanted on the cover of a brochure being handed out to raise funds for a Haitian family that had lost their home in an earthquake. During the collection, the schoolteacher wrote a check for the entire amount she had saved and put it in the basket. When someone asked her how the house-hunting was going, she smiled and said that she had bought the perfect home but that someone else was going to live in it. She added, "I have all I need here. Maybe I will save up and buy another house for someone else."

By practicing generosity daily, you will build up this important spiritual muscle, and you will find that you can more easily love others as God loves you. You will be freer to make a gift of yourself in beautiful, creative, and meaningful ways. To grow in the virtue of generosity, say often this famous prayer by Saint Ignatius of Loyola:

Prayer of Generosity

Eternal Word, only begotten Son of God,
Teach me true generosity.
Teach me to serve you as you deserve.
To give without counting the cost,
To fight heedless of the wounds,
To labor without seeking rest,
To sacrifice myself without thought of any reward
Save the knowledge that I have done your will. Amen.[13]

15

Honor

"For he will render to every man according to his works: to those who by patience in well-doing seek for glory and honor and immortality, he will give eternal life."

—Romans 2:6

The virtue of honor is the habit of recognizing your own dignity and acting accordingly. You are a unique and beloved creation of God. You have been wonderfully made in His image. He knew you before you were born, in your mother's womb. You have been blessed with particular gifts and talents. In acknowledgment of all of this, the honorable person acts with integrity.

You have the ability to choose between right and wrong. You can either make good on your commitments or break them. You can choose to serve others or to ignore them. In every case, you can either act in accord with your dignity or choose not to. This is God's gift of free will. He is a loving Father, not a dictator. You can act either honorably or dishonorably. An honorable person has high standards. He knows who he is and refuses to act in ways that contradict his principles.

Honor and Being Honored

In the ancient world, honor was highly valued. Integrity was one of the most important attributes anyone could have. To be honored by others for honorable conduct was the highest form of praise. Entire plays were written about retaining or regaining one's honor, in other words, one's reputation for having integrity. Nearly every school of philosophy taught that honor was one of the highest pursuits of mankind.

But honor was sometimes pursued for the worldly advantages that often came with it. Being honored and having a good reputation gave a person access to various privileges and served as a kind of credit rating. A man's word was his bond, which is why Jesus said, "Let what you say be simply 'Yes' or 'No'" (Mt 5:37). Thus, sometimes men cared about performing good actions only when others were looking at them and were likely to reward them, as they sometimes do today. But the pursuit of public recognition is not a virtue, and it can often be the vice of pride or vanity.

Vainglory is excessive pride in one's achievements and the inordinate desire for recognition. Saint Thomas Aquinas described three forms of vainglorious ambition: "First, when a man desires recognition of an excellence which he has not: this is to desire more than his share of honor. Secondly, when a man desires honor for himself, without referring it to God. Thirdly, when a man's appetite rests in honor itself, without referring it to the profit of others. Since then ambition denotes an inordinate desire of honor, it is evident that it is always a sin."[1]

When Tom was working on his master's degree in business administration, to push himself toward his goals he would frequently recite in his mind this motivational phrase: "If it is going to be, it is up to me!" While that sounds like a harmless mantra from a self-help book, in Tom's case it fed ambition and stimulated vainglory. By focusing only on his own effort, he ignored the power of God and the vital importance of His grace. After he had an awakening of faith on a retreat in 1997, the aspiring young advertising executive learned that he needed the humility to give God credit for his accomplishments and the honor they would bring him.

Honor as Integrity

When we speak of the virtue of honor, we are speaking of the habit of acting with *integrity*, which means *doing the right thing because it is the right thing, even when no one is watching*. This virtue is seen in the person who keeps his word even when it seems advantageous to break it. It is seen in the courageous men and women who valiantly defend the innocent from injustice, and in the husband who personally cares for his wife suffering from Alzheimer's.

Honor is one of the most desired virtues. People want to act hon-orably because they want to earn the respect and the trust of others. We talk about honor among thieves, meaning that even those who commit crime for a living follow a code of behavior among them-selves. Understanding honor, and seeking to practice this virtue, is important for every person, and especially for Christians, who are supposed to imitate the Lord and lead others to Him.

While we all want to be honored, we do not always live honor-ably. For one thing, we all struggle to keep our word to others. We even struggle to keep commitments to ourselves. We say, "Tomor-row I will clean my room." And then tomorrow comes, and we say, "Nope, not today, my room is not really that messy." Another reason we struggle with integrity is that we see corrupt and dishonest people getting ahead in this world. We are then tempted to rationalize and defend our own sinfulness by thinking that *everyone else does it*. For the person with integrity, doing the right thing is its own reward. But doing the right thing often costs us, and that is when it is particularly difficult to see people rewarded for the wrong thing or honored for the wrong reason. Mark Twain wrote, "It is better to deserve honors and not have them, than to have them and not deserve them."[2] But it is easier to say that than to feel it. Which is why the Old Testament cautions us, "Do not envy the honors of a sinner, for you do not know what his end will be" (Sir 9:11).

Honor in the New Testament

Jesus calls us to do the right thing for the right reason, which is to please God our Father. Jesus warned, "Beware of practicing your piety before men in order to be seen by them; for then you will have no reward from your Father who is in heaven" (Mt 6:1). He went on to say that we should pray, fast, and give alms in secret and that God who sees in secret will reward us (see Mt 6:2–18). Jesus knows that we crave praise and appreciation and that if we are not careful, we can develop the habit of doing good things to receive honor from others and forget about God. Then we are more prone to ignore what we know is right and even do what is wrong in order to please those who can reward us in this world. Jesus asks us to do good things in secret in order to train our wills to do good for the love of God.

Jesus also warned against hypocrisy, which is pretending to have principles or beliefs that one does not have, usually in order to gain wealth or power. He had very harsh words for the hypocrites in his day, the religious leaders who made a big show of their observances of the Jewish law but had no love for God or neighbor. "Woe to you scribes and Pharisees, hypocrites! for you tithe mint and dill and cumin, and have neglected the weightier matters of the law, justice and mercy and faith" (Mt 23:23). These leaders not only said one thing and did another but did not live up to what they claimed was most important to them. In another place, Jesus criticized the Jewish leaders by quoting the prophet Isaiah: "This people honors me with their lips, but their heart is far from me" (Mt 15:8; Is 29:13). Therefore, Jesus said, "practice and observe whatever they tell you, but not what they do; for they preach, but do not practice. They bind heavy burdens, hard to bear, and lay them on men's shoulders; but they themselves will not move them with their finger. They do all their deeds to be seen by men" (Mt 23:3–4). One way to avoid becoming a hypocrite is to follow Jesus' command to do good things in secret so as not to impress anyone.

A Corresponding Beatitude

Another way a person avoids becoming a hypocrite is by being willing to suffer for doing what he says he believes. Jesus said, "Blessed are those who are persecuted for righteousness' sake, for theirs is the kingdom of heaven" (Mt 5:10). Many brave and honorable people have been persecuted for doing the right thing when everyone around them seemed to have forgotten what the right thing is. And while they were suffering for their integrity they were in union with Christ Himself.

On a rainy day in 1955, Rosa Parks boarded a bus after a long day working as a seamstress. She sat in the fifth row, which was the first row of the "colored section". When the bus became full, in order to give the seats nearer the front to white passengers, the bus driver ordered Mrs. Parks and three other African Americans to move to the back of the bus. Rosa Parks didn't move. She quietly sat as the bus driver threatened her. She sat quietly as the police came and arrested her. She didn't know it at the time, but her courageous and honorable act would ignite a series of events that would fuel the civil rights movement. A few days after her arrest, a young and relatively unknown minister, Martin Luther King Jr., would organize the Montgomery Bus Boycott.

Mrs. Parks didn't refuse to sit in the back of the bus because she wanted honors. She did it because refusing to bow to injustice was the honorable thing to do. Acting honorably takes guts. It requires having the courage and the determination to do the right thing, even when others are pressuring you to do the opposite. The old adage says, "Stand for what is right, even if it means standing alone." Having honor often means making sacrifices alone.

In the Old Testament, there is the story of the Maccabees, who resisted the attempts of their pagan rulers to stamp out the Jewish religion. Eleazar, an honorable elderly man in a high position, refused to obey the laws that compromised his faith. When he was arrested, he was given an ultimatum—either eat pork, which is against the Jewish law, or be killed. He not only refused to comply, but also refused to pretend he was complying so as not to set a bad example for others. "By manfully giving up my life now, I will show myself worthy of my old age and leave to the young a noble example of how to die a good death willingly and nobly for the revered and holy laws" (2 Mac 6:27–28).

Eleazar paid the ultimate price for his convictions. He knew who he was and what he was about, and at ninety years old he was not going to offend God in order to live a few more years. We might suppose that this decision would have been harder for a younger man. But among the Maccabees were other martyrs, including a heroic mother and her seven sons. Having honor means knowing what, or who, is worthy of sacrifice, beginning with God Himself. It was not Eleazar's stubbornness that made him honorable, it was his knowledge of what is most important.

Christian Honor

Ask yourself, now, what is most important to you. For what are you willing to lay down your life? If captured by a radical jihadist, would you deny your Christian faith in order to live?

It is said that you can't give your honor away, but you can lose it. In the military, losing your honor means failing to have lived up to the expectations of service within your rank. And that applies to us too. However, for the Christian, having honor is more than just keeping your word, fulfilling your obligations, and being a generally good person. It means living in accord with the truth of who we are as children of God. Pope Saint John XXIII was one of the most respected leaders of his time for his constant invitation to aspire to what is best in ourselves. He said, "Christ's Church is, above all, the spiritual temple where every Christian knows he has his place: he knows he has it, and he is aware of his duty to keep it with honor, dignity, and grace."[3]

For Christians, living honorably means following Christ even at the risk of persecution and death. Down through the centuries, many Christians have failed to live up to their calling. In times of persecution, many Christians have compromised their faith out of fear not only for their lives but for their livelihoods, property, and status. But the most beautiful thing about being a Christian is that when you fall, you do not need to rationalize it; you only need to repent and get up again. "For a righteous man falls seven times, and rises again" (Prov 24:16).

In a Catholics Come Home Evangomercial, legendary Hall of Fame football coach Lou Holtz summarized how to live honorably as a Catholic Christian:

> For victory in life, we've got to keep focused on the goal, and the goal is Heaven. The key to winning is choosing to do God's will and love others with all you've got. Sacrifice, discipline and prayer are essential. We gain strength through God's Word, and we receive Grace from the sacraments. And when we fumble due to sin, and it's *gonna* happen, Confession puts us back on the field. So if you haven't been to church weekly, get back in the game. We're saving your starting seat on the bench this Sunday![4]

Being honorable does not mean never making a mistake or never doing something wrong. Rather, it means having the humility to admit that we have a lot to learn—from God, from others, and even from our missteps—before we can become great at anything and be worthy of honor. "The fear of the LORD is instruction in wisdom, and humility goes before honor" (Prov 15:33).

Saint Josemaría Escrivá served as a priest during the Spanish Civil War, when Catholics were persecuted for their faith and some were even killed. He founded Opus Dei to help people find ways of sanctifying their everyday life. He said, "The saint is not the person who never fails, but rather the one who never fails to get up again, humbly and with a holy stubbornness."[5] The 1990s Christian singer Bob Carlisle popularized this teaching with the song "We Fall Down": "We fall down, we get up. And the saints are just the sinners who fall down and get up."[6] Getting up again takes not only humility but also courage, because sometimes the bad decisions we make and their consequences are very grave indeed.

The Example of King David

Often when people see the fall of a great man, they assume that he is a hypocrite. But sometimes people fail to live up to their own standards not because they don't believe them, but because they were weak.

Kind David, one of the most celebrated leaders in history, messed up badly. He had a soldier in his army killed to cover up his affair with the man's wife, Bathsheba. The Lord sent David's friend Nathan to confront him about his sinful actions. He posed a parable to King David:

> There were two men in a certain city, the one rich and the other poor. The rich man had very many flocks and herds; but the poor man had nothing but one little ewe lamb, which he had bought. And he brought it up, and it grew up with him and with his children; . . . and it was like a daughter to him. Now there came a traveler to the rich man, and he was unwilling to take one of his own flock or herd to prepare for the wayfarer who had come to him, but he took the poor man's lamb, and prepared it for the man. (2 Sam 12:1–4)

David was outraged at the callousness and the injustice of the rich man, and he said, "As the LORD lives, the man who has done this deserves to die; and he shall restore the lamb fourfold, because he did this thing, and because he had no pity" (2 Sam 12:5–6). Nathan replied, "You are the man." Then he listed all the ways the Lord had blessed David and explained how the Lord would punish him. And David said to Nathan, "I have sinned against the LORD." He didn't make excuses, he didn't defend his actions, he didn't blame God for making Bathsheba so darn beautiful. No, he confessed his sin. And Nathan told David that he had been forgiven, "The LORD also has put away your sin; you shall not die." Instead David's son born to Bath-sheba would die (2 Sam 12:7–15).

David repented, accepted the consequences of his actions, and mourned his sinfulness. It was in this period that he wrote Psalm 51:

> Create in me a clean heart, O God,
>   and put a new and right spirit within me....
> Restore to me the joy of your salvation,
>   and uphold me with a willing spirit.
> Then I will teach transgressors your ways,
>   and sinners will return to you....
> The sacrifice acceptable to God is a broken spirit;
>   a broken and contrite heart, O God, you will not despise.
>   (vv. 10–13, 17)

These are not the words of a hypocrite, who says things he does not believe, but of an honorable man truly sorry for the wrong he has done.

Honor and the Saints

There are many stories of saints honorably upholding their convictions even when threatened with death. Saint Thomas More, the chancellor of England under King Henry VIII, was imprisoned in the Tower of London and then executed for refusing to swear an oath to the king that would make him the head of the church in England. He went to his death saying, "I die the king's good servant, and God's first."[7]

In the third century, during the persecution of Christians under Roman Emperor Diocletian, Saint Agnes would not break her vow to remain a virgin for the Lord by marrying one of her pagan suitors. One or more of them betrayed her to the authorities, and she was arrested, beaten brutally, and killed.

Many more saints, known to us and unknown, had such great honor that they would rather be imprisoned, tortured, or killed than to compromise what they knew God was asking them to do. Most of us won't be faced with dying for our honor as martyrs, but we are given other opportunities large and small to choose what we know is right, to defend it, and to live as people with integrity even when it causes us suffering of some kind.

Honor and the Temperaments

Choleric

People with a choleric temperament are motivated by action. They are doers and love to respond to a challenge. Cholerics can easily sacrifice for a worthy goal. However, they can be prone to pride and self-righteousness. They need to seek honor in humility and not fall into the trap of vainglory, which is excessively seeking public recognition. They also need to give honor and glory to God for all of their accomplishments and to share honor with others who have helped them along the way.

Sanguine

People with a sanguine temperament love people and are motivated by relationships. They are capable of doing heroic and honorable things in service to others. However, they often struggle with wanting to be the center of attention and may lack perseverance. They need to seek honor with humility along with the courage to persevere and the self-control to subdue their appetite for pleasurable diversions.

Phlegmatic

People with a phlegmatic temperament are motivated by peace. They have a keen sense of justice and are naturally drawn toward healing and restoring the brokenness they encounter. For this reason, many phlegmatics are honored for their work in peace-building and diplomacy. However, they tend toward inaction and passivity and need to be courageous in defending what they know is right even if it creates conflict and discord with others.

Melancholic

People with a melancholic temperament are motivated by ideas. They tend to be deep and have rich interior lives. They can live and defend their core beliefs and be unwilling to compromise them. They tend to value honor more than the other temperaments do. However, they often doubt their own strength and their own ability to contribute to the challenges they face. They need to practice courage, especially audacity, in order to do the honorable actions they are inspired to do.

Associated Virtues

The virtue of honor is assisted and practiced more readily when accompanied by these other virtues.

- *Self-worth* is knowing that you are an unrepeatable and unique gift to the world.
- *Proper pride* is being proud of what you have accomplished with God's help.
- *Loyalty* is keeping one's commitments to family, friends, and colleagues.
- *Integrity* is acting in ways that are consistent with who you are and what you say you believe.
- *Responsibility* is taking ownership of actions both good and bad and accepting their consequences.

Associated Vices

A lack of honor can manifest itself in many ways, and we must be careful of these vices in order to be honorable people.

- Vanity—admiring yourself too much, especially your physical appearance. *Steals the joy of serving others and sharing one's blessings.*
- Vainglory—excessively seeking attention, praise, and honor. *Steals the joy of being properly esteemed and rewarded by God alone.*
- Small-mindedness—thinking too little of yourself and resigning yourself to being mediocre. *Steals the joy of seeking greatness and believing in yourself.*
- Envy—resenting the possessions or the successes of others. *Steals the joy of being happy for others.*
- Laziness—failing to give the situation the attention and the effort it deserves. *Steals your ability to use your particular gifts to serve others.*
- Cowardice—avoiding noble, necessary battles for fear of what they might cost. *Steals your ability to defend heroically what is good, beautiful, and true.*

Practical Ways to Grow

That's the textbook stuff, but let us talk for a moment about honor in action, and what it takes to develop this virtue at work, at home, and in life. To have honor, a person needs three things:

1. A desire to have integrity in speech.
2. A desire to have integrity in action.
3. A personal commitment to doing the right thing for the right reason no matter the cost.

Christians are called to be honorable people who seek to do what is right, just, and compassionate. Christians should admit their short-comings when they fail and resolve to do better. The constant prayer of the Christian should be "Lord, work through me, more than you have to work in spite of me."

Want to live more honorably? Here's how in five easy steps.

1. Think of all the people in your life you want your actions to honor. First and foremost, you want to honor and glorify God. After that, you want to bring honor to your mom and dad, your wife or husband, your third grade teacher, your best

friend, your pastor, your grandpa, and so on. Think of these people. These are the people you want your actions to reflect well upon. Are you seeking to live in a way that honors their love and care for you?

2. Think of the commitments in your life. Your marriage, your fatherhood or motherhood, your friendships, your church community, your job. What does fulfilling these commitments look like? What does it mean to be a committed husband or wife, and so on? What does it mean to fulfill your obligations to your work? What does it look like to live out the precepts of your faith by being a committed member of the Church?

3. Think of your relationship with God. Are you honoring His commandments? Are you honoring the gifts He has given you (your family, your spouse, your children, your friends, etc.)? Are you honoring the mission God has given you?

4. Now that you've thought about these things, have a serious conversation with God in prayer. Are you honoring the people in your life with your actions? Are you honoring your commitments? And, above all, are you honoring God?

5. Now that you have thought about it and talked to God about it, thank God for all the opportunities He has given you and the ways that you are succeeding in honoring those people and commitments. Ask God for opportunities to practice the other virtues, so that you may live more honorably.

Imagine if you brought these five steps to your daily prayer and your discernment process. Imagine if you let these five steps determine how you were succeeding in life. Being honorable to your family is far more important than what type of car you drive or what brand of clothes you wear. Think about it. Let your integrity be your yardstick of success.

By practicing the virtue of honor, and seeking to have integrity daily, you will build up this important spiritual muscle. You will find it easier to honor your commitments and to serve the people in your life. You will be freer to make a gift of yourself to whatever noble battles God may call you to fight.

16

Greatheartedness

"Truly, truly, I say to you, he who believes in me will also do the works that I do; and greater works than these will he do."

—John 14:12

The virtue of greatheartedness (or magnanimity) is the habit of knowing that you are called to do great things and daring to do them with confidence. It is the virtue of great hearts and great minds who seek to achieve good and noble ends. The ancient world highly esteemed this virtue, and when someone did something heroic and selfless, people would say, "Of course, that person has a great heart!" The Athenian philosophers admired magnanimity as evidence of a virtuous life, calling it the crown of virtue. The Stoics held it as the virtue befitting great people.

Christian Magnanimity

For the Christian, the virtue of greatheartedness begins in knowing that you have been created by God in His image. This is the source of your dignity. Even on a purely biological level you are amazing. Seriously, even with all the shortcomings you may have, all the knocks you may have received along the way, you can say with Psalm 139, "I am wondrously made" (v. 14). You are composed of more than thirty trillion cells working together through complex processes to run all of the systems of an incredible living being. You also have a mind that can process all of the information coming in through all of your senses and that can remember and interpret millions of experiences both good and bad. Now consider that the God of the universe who created everything, and everything with a purpose, has created you with a free will so that you can choose to act as He does.

God has placed you in this world in a certain place and a certain time and with a certain mission. And, on top of all of this, He loves you! He loves you just the way you are, but way too much to leave you that way. He is reaching out to you as a loving father reaches out to his wayward son (see Lk 15:11–32) and as a mother comforts her child (see Is 66:13). Your dignity does not come from what you do or how well you do it. You could be in a coma in an intensive care unit and you would have exactly the same dignity you have now. As a Christian your dignity comes not from doing but from being loved into existence by God and joined to His Church through Baptism. And yet, the knowledge of this dignity is what prompts greathearted Christians to do great things for God, as a response to His love. In fact, every Christian, aware of his or her dignity as a son or a daughter of God, should seek nothing less than greatness. All Christians should seek to mirror Christ through cooperation with God's calling and grace.

Greatheartedness and Pride

Over the centuries Christian sages and saints have warned against the pride that can either cause or result from a misguided desire for greatness. While Christians must avoid pride, they are nevertheless called by Christ to "be perfect, therefore, as your heavenly Father is perfect" (Mt 5:48). The Church affirms that the way we attain the perfection God intends for us is by participating in Christ's mission to reveal God's love for the world. How? By cooperating with His grace in order to continue His work on earth, as He commanded His apostles before He returned to the Father: "Go therefore and make disciples of all nations" (Mt 28:19).

Christian greatheartedness is not pride. First of all, accepting God's mercy requires the humble recognition that we need it. Second, the desire to serve and to glorify God by helping to spread His kingdom on earth requires another form of humility—gratitude. Everyone is tempted to be proud, and we discuss this vice and its antidote, humility, in chapter 12. Here let us say that one way to keep greatheartedness humble is by practicing this virtue as Alexandre Havard describes it: "Seeking greatness by bringing out the greatness in others."[1] In other words, to be truly greathearted you must also want others to be great. This means helping others to be aware of their dignity and encouraging them to use their talents to do great things for God. This insight is key to avoiding pride in your pursuits or envy of other's achievements.

Small-mindedness

The enemy of greatheartedness is small-mindedness. A better but less common word is *pusillanimity*, which means "small-souledness", "weakness", "cowardliness", or "wishy-washyness". It is the exact opposite of the word *magnanimity*, which literally means "great-souledness". Small-souledness, or small-mindedness, is not just fear or timidity. Fear and timidity are normal responses to dangerous situations and are sometimes good for protecting us. Smart people ought to fear challenges for which they are not ready. Small-mindedness, on the other hand, is habitually telling yourself that "you can't" when in actual fact you can if you make the effort. Small-mindedness defeats us before we even begin. It prevents us from even preparing ourselves to meet challenges.

Small-mindedness is based on a lie that directly attacks your dignity and your ability to do great things for others and for God. The devil often puffs up our pride in order to turn us away from serving God and others. But when that doesn't work, he sometimes attacks our confidence in our dignity as children of God, telling us that we are incapable of great acts of service. But "with God all things are possible" (Mt 19:26). As Saint Paul said, "I can do all things in him who strengthens me" (Phil 4:13).

In truth, the gifts that we have been given are never just for us. They are meant to glorify God and to serve others. Pusillanimity, small-mindedness, prevents us from developing and sharing those gifts, causing us to miss opportunities for doing good. Think of the small-minded servant in the Parable of the Talents, who buried the one coin he was given instead of putting it to use (see Mt 25:14–30). At the end of the story Jesus warned, "To every one who has will more be given, and he will have abundance; but from him who has not, even what he has will be taken away" (v. 29). Greatheartedness adds to the goodness and the bounty of the world, while small-mindedness subtracts from it.

Pride and Vanity

The other enemies of Christian greatheartedness are prideful ambition and vanity. Seeking to do great things on your own, without discerning God's will for you, in order to look great in your own eyes or to gain fame or fortune, is a sign that you are motivated by pride or vanity. Saint Thomas Aquinas devoted a whole chapter in the *Summa* to this topic. There is a fine line between being ambitious for self-gain and being ambitious in responding to your calling from God. The difference lies in what your final goal is. Is your goal to like your own reflection in the mirror, to be honored by other people, or to have wealth and power? Or is it to fulfill your God-given mission, regardless of whether anyone else knows what you have achieved and rewards you for it? Greatheartedness is the virtue between the vice of excessively performing on one hand and the vice of underperforming on the other. It is doing what God asks, no more and no less, with all you have to give. And when we do, we become the men and women God created us to be, in spite of our faults. As we have quoted previously, "*We are not the sum of our weaknesses and failures*; we are the sum of the Father's love for us and our real capacity to become the image of His Son."[2]

The goal of the Christian is to become like Christ, and there is nothing greater than that. As Pope Benedict XVI said, "Man was created for greatness—for God Himself; he was created to be filled by God. But his heart is too small for the greatness to which it is destined. It must be stretched."[3] Growing in the virtue of greatheartedness means allowing ourselves to be stretched in order to fit into the greatness God wills for us. From this perspective, we see that our bad habits and sins are too small for us, and our desire to replace them with virtues grows.

Examples of Greatheartedness

Heroes of both the ancient and modern worlds are greathearted individuals keenly aware that they were made for some special purpose. As Saint John Henry Newman wrote,

> [God] has committed some work to me which He has not committed to another. I have my mission—I may never know it in this life, but I shall be told it in the next. . . . I am a link in a chain, a bond of connection between persons. He has not created me for naught. I shall do good; I shall do His work. . . . if I do but keep His commandments and serve Him in my calling. . . . Therefore I will trust Him. Whatever, wherever I am, I can never be thrown away. . . . He does nothing in vain. . . . He knows what He is about.[4]

These are the words of a greathearted person.

The lay evangelist and founder of Prison Fellowship, Chuck Colson, wrote, "It is men and women, under [God's] jurisdiction, who write the pages of history through the sum of their choices. We never know what minor act of hopeless courage, what word spoken in defense of truth, what unintended consequence might swing the balance and change the world. . . . History pivots on the actions of individuals, both great and ordinary."[5] He pointed to the example of Queen Esther, whose memory is venerated in both Judaism and Christianity. When her uncle urged her to plead with her husband, the king, to save her people from destruction, Queen Esther was afraid. Then her uncle exhorted her by saying, "Who knows whether you have not come to the kingdom for such a time as this?" (Esther 4:14). Esther did not seek a noble deed to accomplish, but when God asked one of her, she agreed and placed herself in His hands.

One day a young boy named Coley Taylor told Mark Twain how much he enjoyed *Huckleberry Finn* and *Tom Sawyer*. To Coley's surprise, Twain wagged his finger and said, "You shouldn't read those books about bad boys!" Twain continued, "Now listen to what an old man tells you. My best book is my *Recollections of Joan of Arc*. You are too young to understand and enjoy it now, but read it when you are older. Remember then what I tell you now. *Joan of Arc* is my very best book."[6]

Why did one of the greatest American authors respond to young Coley Taylor in such a way? After all, *Huckleberry Finn* and *Tom Sawyer* are two of Twain's most beloved classics! And they are classics because they portray the reality of life as we know it, peppered with vivid detail, exuberant humor, and wandering imagination. However, his novel about Saint Joan of Arc portrays life ideally, as it could be if we would live in accord with our greatness. Twain understood this difference.

Joan of Arc has fascinated many authors, not just Mark Twain, because her story is incredible. She was a peasant girl from northern France who was inspired by God to awaken the faith and the hope of the French during the Hundred Years' War. They had forgotten who they were and were dejected after losing many battles to the English.

While northern France was under English control, young Joan began having mystical visions inspiring her to greater piety and love for God. Eventually, she believed that God was calling her to help the French army win back the country. With no knowledge about using weapons or even riding a horse, Joan knew not how she would achieve this mission, yet she sought a meeting with the heir to the throne, Charles. After a long conversation with Joan and her examination by his counselors, Charles gave the seventeen-year-old armor and a horse and allowed her to accompany the army to the besieged city of Orleans, which they liberated from the English. Joan led the French to further victories, which allowed Charles to be crowned the king of France.

Allies of the English captured Joan and turned her over to them, and they tried her for heresy and burned her at the stake. But she had captured the imagination of the entire nation by bringing out greatness in the men she led. She also had changed the hearts of her fellow countrymen, calling them to deeper prayer and trust in God. Mark Twain pointed out that she was the only person, of either sex, who ever held supreme command of the military forces of a nation at the age of seventeen. For Twain, this was because Joan of Arc was an exemplary greathearted person.

Greatheartedness is the virtue of men and women who seek to make a gift of themselves to God by saying yes to His plan for them. Father Lawrence Lovasik, S.V.D., said that "[our] mission in life should be to reconquer for God's glory His unhappy world, and give it back to Him".[7] We need the virtue of greatheartedness to say yes to that mission.

A Corresponding Beatitude

Greatheartedness is the central virtue of the Christian life because it is the virtue we need in order to follow Christ and to live, as He did, according to all of the beatitudes. The first thing Jesus asks is that we follow Him, and it takes a great heart to say yes. As Pope Benedict XVI said,

> Christ did not promise an easy life.... Rather, he shows us the way to great things, the good, towards an authentic human life....
> When he speaks of the cross that we ourselves have to carry,... [i]t is the impulse of love, which has its own momentum and does not seek itself but opens the person to the service of truth, justice and the good. Christ shows God to us, and thus the true greatness of man.[8]

We need greatheartedness not only to answer the call of Jesus to follow Him but also to cooperate with His grace to grow in whatever virtues we need to fulfill the unique mission He gives to us. We might not ever be called to do anything great in the eyes of the world, but we are greathearted if we agree to grow into the virtuous man or woman God intends us to be. "Magnanimity is sometimes called the 'adornment' of all the other virtues," explained theologian Edward Sri, "for the magnanimous man endeavors to make his virtues greater."[9] And the Christian endeavors to do this in order to serve the Lord.

Greatheartedness and the Temperaments

Choleric

People with a choleric temperament have lots of energy and seek to accomplish big things. They are capable of large undertakings that require strength and endurance. They tend to have an awareness of their abilities and can do things with great enthusiasm. However, their propensity to act can mean they fail to discern properly the action needed and their role in it. To avoid blind activism, the choleric needs to cultivate humility and prudence in order to do the right thing, at the right time, for the right reason, and with the right attitude.

Sanguine

People with the sanguine temperament love people and are motivated by relationships. They also love adventure and can be greathearted when starting a new endeavor. They can champion and begin worthy projects and tasks. However, they sometimes lack the patience to reflect sufficiently and plan accordingly. They may lack endurance and may falter in the actions necessary to accomplish the mission. To be greathearted, sanguines need to discern the demands of the task and their readiness for it. They need to cultivate the ability to endure suffering in order to persevere in a worthy mission.

Phlegmatic

People with the phlegmatic temperament are motivated by peace. They have a keen sense of justice and are naturally drawn toward healing and restoring any brokenness they encounter. Phlegmatics prefer to keep the status quo and avoid conflict. They willingly compromise for the sake of unity and peace and can conform themselves to those around them. They tend not to initiate action. To be greathearted, they need to learn how to take risks in order to achieve the noble and worthy things they desire. They need to accept that they will never have certainty of an outcome but that they can have enough information to act prudently.

Melancholic

People with the melancholic temperament are motivated by ideas. They tend to be deep and have rich interior lives. They are good at analyzing situations and can help provide the information needed for greathearted action. They are aware of their own dignity and talents, and they seek noble and worthy goals. However, like the phlegmatic, they struggle with taking action. They fear failure and are averse to risk. To be greathearted, the melancholic needs to make it his personal mission to act upon his good and noble aspirations to serve God and others.

Associated Virtues

The virtue of greateartedness is assisted and practiced more readily when accompanied by these other virtues.

- *Self-Awareness* is knowing your own strengths and weaknesses.
- *Honor* is knowing your own dignity and acting accordingly.
- *Courage* is bravely responding to what each situation demands.

Associated Vices

A lack of greateartedness can manifest itself in many ways, and we must be careful of these vices in order to grow in this virtue.

- Cowardice—being crippled by the "what ifs". *Steals your ability to engage in noble battle and the joy of suffering for worthy causes.*
- False humility—denying your abilities because of pretense, low self-esteem, or false notions of humility. *Steals the joy of striving to be the best person you can be.*
- Pride—thinking too highly of yourself. Denying the truth about your weaknesses. *Steals the joy of serving others and sharing one's blessings.*
- Envy—resenting the possessions or the successes of others. *Steals the joy of sharing in someone else's joy.*
- Laziness—failing to give the situation the attention and the effort it deserves. *Steals the joy of being in right relationship with others and growing in trust and friendship.*

Practical Ways to Grow

That's the textbook stuff but let us talk for a moment about real greateartedness in action, and what it takes to develop this virtue at

work, at home, and in life. To have greatheartedness, a person needs
to do these four things:

1. Believe that you are called to greatness.
2. Surround yourself with great and noble things.
3. Be willing serve God and others in both small and big ways.
4. Be willing to sacrifice and suffer for what is good, beautiful, and
   true.

Practice being greathearted by thinking about great and noble
things: real love, true friendship, and honorable sacrifice. Surround
yourself with stories, music, movies, and people who *aspire* to make
a positive and real difference in the world and *inspire* you to do
the same.

As a former national media executive, Tom understands how so
much of the secular media we consume directs our attention to our
immediate wants, pleasures, and fantasies. If we listen to music that
constantly subjugates women, chances are we will have that same
attitude and start to treat women as objects. If we read romance nov-
els that are less about love and more about lust, chances are we'll start
to think of sex only as pleasure and not as a gift of self. The truth is
that we often emulate the messages that surround us. We must curate
and consume good media and good messages that support who we
really are and challenge us to become better people. We are what
we eat, so lay off the junk media and surround yourself with healthy
and spiritually uplifting books, people, and music in order to find real
purpose and true happiness.

Saint Catherine of Siena said, "Be who God meant you to be and
you will set the world on fire."[10] Matthew Kelly, a popular author
and inspiring speaker, often says that we should seek "to be the best
version of ourselves". Think about it. Imagine the best version of
yourself. Would you be more patient, more loving, more responsive
to the needs of your spouse, children, family, friends, and so on?
Would you be less angry in traffic, more forgiving of your colleagues,
less annoyed by silly and trivial things? Believe it or not, this is the
start of greatheartedness.

First, surround yourself with people and things that elevate your
mind toward great ideas and noble aspirations. Second, act nobly and

selflessly in service to God and others in small and ordinary ways. Third, seek to be great by calling out greatness in others. Fourth, give God permission to use you in His plan for the world.

Greatheartedness always grows and is strengthened alongside the virtues of honor and courage. Practice greatheartedness by courageously and honorably completing your daily tasks and seeking to serve God and others in both large and small ways. By practicing greatheartedness daily, you will build up this important spiritual muscle, and you will be more capable of great and noble things. You will be freer and more prepared to love and to be a hero in the story that God has written for your life!

17

Gratitude

"O give thanks to the LORD, for he is good;
for his mercy endures for ever!"

—Psalm 106:1

The virtue of gratitude is the habit of being thankful for all that you have. Gratitude begins with being thankful for your life and the lives of those you have depended on, starting with your parents. Next we are thankful for all of our abilities and all the gifts of the earth that we use each day to provide for ourselves and our families. Then there are the many gifts we receive throughout our lives, some large, some wrapped for special occasions, and some small but meaningful. An embrace of a friend, a smile from a stranger, a helping hand in a time in need—for these also we give thanks.

Because we have free will, we can choose not to give. Because giving is a choice, we ought to be thankful when someone chooses to share something with us. Having the virtue of gratitude means recognizing, honoring, and thanking those who have shared something of themselves with you, starting with God.

Thanking God

Gratitude starts with thanking God for the gift of your life. God does not need us, but He freely chose to create us. He created each and every one of us in His image as a unique, unrepeatable, beloved son or daughter. Furthermore, He reveals Himself to us—through His creation and, most intimately, by becoming one of us in His Son, Jesus Christ.

We also thank God for the gift of salvation. Though we are sinners, He does not abandon us but removes our sins by taking them upon Himself. "But God shows his love for us in that while we were yet sinners Christ died for us" (Rom 5:8). God forgives our sins so that we can have new life in Him. "I came that you may have life, and have it abundantly" (Jn 10:10).

Thanking God is not something we do in the abstract. There are concrete and personal ways we can show God our gratitude for creating us, revealing Himself to us, providing for us, and forgiving us.

Gratitude in the Gospels

There is perhaps no sweeter gratitude than that which comes from a truly penitent sinner who has been forgiven. One night, while Jesus was dining at the home of a Pharisee, "a woman of the city, who was a sinner" interrupted their meal. She wept with remorse for her sins and bathed Jesus' feet with her tears. She wiped His feet with her hair, kissed them, and anointed them with ointment from an alabaster flask.

The Pharisee wondered how Jesus could let this sinful woman touch Him. Reading the man's thoughts, Jesus said, "A certain creditor had two debtors; one owed five hundred denarii, and the other fifty. When they could not pay, he forgave them both. Now which of them will love him more?" The Pharisee answered, "The one, I suppose, to whom he forgave more." And Jesus said, "You have judged rightly." Then he explained that the woman's gestures, which outdid anything the Pharisee had done for Jesus, were proof of her great love. And her love was the result of God forgiving her many sins. Jesus said, "He who is forgiven little, loves little" (Lk 7:36–47). But don't we all need as much forgiveness as this sinful woman? Is Jesus implying that our pride blinds us to our need for God's mercy and blocks us from loving Him?

Another illuminating example of gratitude is seen when Jesus heals ten lepers.

As he entered a village, he was met by ten lepers, who stood at a distance and lifted up their voices and said, "Jesus, Master, have mercy on us." When he saw them he said to them, "Go and show yourselves to the priests." And as they went they were cleansed. Then one of them, when he saw that he was healed, turned back, praising God with a loud voice; and he fell on his face at Jesus' feet, giving him thanks. Now he was a Samaritan. Then said Jesus, "Were not ten cleansed? Where are the nine? Was no one found to return and give praise to God except this foreigner?" (Lk 17:11–19).

Could this be the case with us? That only one in every ten of us acknowledge all that God does for us and thank Him for it?

One way to avoid being like the proud Pharisee or the nine ungrateful lepers is to make a habit of thanking God for even the smallest of blessings. Tom's mom would often pray for a parking space, but more than that, she would thank God when she found one. In contrast is the joke about the guy who prayed and prayed for a parking place, and then when he saw one said, "Never mind, Lord, I just found one!" How many times do we ask God for things but forget to thank Him when He sends them our way? Too many. That's why we need to work on the virtue of gratitude by thanking God for everything rather than thinking our blessings are our own doing.

Counting Your Blessings

The virtue of gratitude is practiced and strengthened whenever we are thankful for our many blessings. So let's review what those blessings are.

The People in Our Life

Consider how often others are making a gift of themselves to you. We should be thankful whenever someone uses his talents to help us, shares his resources with us, or makes time for us. The famous quotes that "No man is an island" and "It takes a village to raise a child" come to mind. We would not even be here if our parents had not brought us into the world and raised us. We would know very little if our teachers had not educated us or our employers and mentors had not trained us.

Consider also your family members and friends who make your life richer and more meaningful. We are created to love and be loved, and for that we need others who help to make us who we are. When we are thankful for them, we treat them better and find more joy in our relationships. So rejoice in others and be thankful for them.

The Things We Have

When considering the good things we have, we should start with our own bodies. Where would we be without our eyes and ears, our arms and legs, our brain? Those of us with good health can easily take these blessings for granted. But even when our senses and strength diminish or are taken away, we can still be grateful for whatever we have, for life itself is a blessing. We have so many examples of incredible people with disabilities—Helen Keller, Joni Eareckson Tada, and Ray Charles, to name a few—who prove that we have gifts to share even when we are physically challenged in some way.

No matter how rich or poor we may be, we have material possessions that provide for our needs and give us pleasure. Our home, our food, our clothes, and even our gadgets are blessings. When we appreciate them, we take good care of them and use them appropriately for the benefit of not just ourselves but others too. Take stock for a moment of all that you have. Praise God for these good things in your life and the joy they bring you and others.

Our Experiences

All of your experiences have formed you and have contributed to the person you are. Going camping, falling in love, traveling to another country—every experience teaches us so much. Even unpleasant experiences—losing a game, getting fired, suffering from a broken heart—teach us important lessons. Bob Goff, a former lawyer who is a philanthropist and a motivational speaker, has explained that all of our experiences, good and "bad", have been formative: "I used to think I could shape the circumstances around me, but now I know Jesus uses circumstances to shape me."[1]

Some experiences are easy to be thankful for. When our heart is full of joy, gratitude just spills out, as it does at the birth of a child or a graduation. Times of trial are usually harder to be thankful for, especially in the middle of them. In hindsight, however, we see that these experiences are often some of the most formative. The pain and struggle are temporary, but the lessons last. "For the moment all discipline seems painful rather than pleasant; later it yields the peaceful fruit of righteousness to those who have been trained by it" (Heb 12:11).

According to Goff, we need God's perspective in order to evaluate our successes and failures: "God finds us in our failures and our successes, and He says that while we used to think one way about those things, now He wants us to think another way about those same things. And for me, I realized that I used to be afraid of failing at the things that really mattered to me, but now I am more afraid of succeeding at things that do not matter."[2] It takes great trust in God to believe in His goodness and try to see things His way when, in the words of a Laura Story song, your "blessings come through raindrops" and "your healing comes through tears."[3]

Old Testament Examples

The Old Testament book of Job illustrates the challenge of praising God in the midst of great suffering. Job loses everything—his property, his children, and his health. His wife scolds him, and his friends torment him by saying that God must be punishing him for his sins. While Job laments his fate, he continues to praise God: "Naked I came from my mother's womb, and naked shall I return; the LORD gave, and the LORD has taken away; blessed be the name of the LORD" (Job 1:20–21). The dialogue between Job and God in chapters 38 through 42 is one of the best summaries of God's power and abiding love, and the need for our humility. God speaks to Job "out of the whirlwind" (38:1). Life is full of storms, and while it is hard to praise God in the middle of one, the story of Job shows us that God uses storms to speak to us and bring about His will for our good.

Joseph is another example of God working through the messiness of life, including human sinfulness. Joseph was sold into slavery by his jealous brothers and ended up in Egypt. After being falsely accused of a crime, he was sent to prison. Throughout his sufferings, Joseph remained steadfast in his faith and trust in God.

It was Joseph's imprisonment that God used to do something amazing. In jail Joseph met some servants of Pharaoh and correctly interpreted their dreams. Pharaoh heard of it and asked Joseph to interpret one of his dreams. Pleased with Joseph, Pharaoh appointed him to a high position in his government—to prepare the nation's food supply for a coming famine.

During the famine, Joseph's brothers arrived in Egypt seeking to purchase grain. They did not recognize Joseph, and he put them through several ordeals to test their integrity. After they proved their remorse for what they had done to him and their love for their father and youngest brother, Joseph revealed himself to them. He assured them of his forgiveness saying, "Do not be distressed, or angry with yourselves, because you sold me here; for God sent me before you to preserve life" (Gen 45:5).

As Saint Paul said, "We know that in everything God works for good with those who love him, who are called according to his purpose" (Rom 8:28). Thus, even in trials, we are called to be thankful. Saint Paul also said, "Rejoice always, pray constantly, give thanks in all circumstances" (1 Thess 5:16–18). "And after you have suffered a little while," said Saint Peter, "the God of all grace, who has called you to his eternal glory in Christ, will himself restore, establish, and strengthen you" (1 Pet 5:10). Just as He did for Job and Joseph, so He does for us.

The Enemies of Gratitude

Why is it so hard to be thankful sometimes? Being thankful is a choice; ultimately gratitude is a virtue and must be practiced. There are real challenges that make choosing to be thankful hard. One challenge is our own pride. Sometimes we think that we deserve all we have because we produced it ourselves. While we all work hard for our accomplishments and possessions, nevertheless our strengths and abilities, our smarts and education are all gifts from God made possible by the many people who have generously helped us.

Sometimes we are ungrateful because we are focused more on the difficult things in life than on our blessings. In the book of Exodus we see that soon after God delivered His people from slavery in

Egypt, they began to worry about their lack of food and water. And after God provided manna and quail each day, they grew tired of this diet and complained about it. Worrying and complaining, which are forms of ingratitude, are very easy to do. The cure for them is to put our trust in God, and when we do, it is easier to be thankful for His providence, steadfastness, and forgiveness. Billy Graham reminds us that "grumbling and gratitude are, for the child of God, in conflict. Be grateful and you won't grumble. Grumble and you won't be grateful . . . praise God in all things."[4]

We can even rejoice in our trials and sufferings, trusting that these too can produce good in our lives if we let them. Saint Paul said, "We have peace with God through our Lord Jesus Christ. Through him we have obtained access to this grace in which we stand, and we rejoice in our hope of sharing the glory of God. More than that, we rejoice in our sufferings, knowing that suffering produces endurance, and endurance produces character, and character produces hope, and hope does not disappoint us, because God's love has been poured into our hearts through the Holy Spirit who has been given to us" (Rom 5:1–5).

Related to our trials in life is another challenge to gratitude: our woundedness. Sometimes the hard knocks we receive leave deep wounds that make it hard for us to trust the goodness of God and others. This lack of trust might affect only certain areas of our lives, like intimate relationships, or it might affect the way we perceive everything. Either way, the wounds at the root of our lack of trust need to be healed through forgiveness—either by accepting God's mercy and forgiving ourselves for what we have done, or by sharing God's mercy with others by forgiving what they have done to us. Sometimes we need spiritual help, professional help, or the help of support groups and programs to heal the wounds left by traumatic experiences, but in the meanwhile, we can still practice the virtue of gratitude by choosing to being thankful for our lives and for all that we have. We carry wounds, but they don't define us; and in time the scars can heal.

Last but not least is the enemy of all spiritual healing and growth, the devil. Full of pride the devil is incapable of gratitude. There is a real spiritual component to the virtues as we have noted elsewhere in this book. Cartoons like to show the drama of spiritual warfare with a good angel on one shoulder and a bad angel, or demon, on the other. The angel speaks truth and the demon speaks lies. While that image might be oversimplified and cliché, it is nonetheless true. We really do hear competing voices of good and evil.

It is important not to overspiritualize the virtues. Properly understood, good habits are developed through practice. The devil doesn't want us to develop any virtues and uses false promises to lure us away from the efforts required to obtain them. However, when it comes to gratitude, the devil makes a full-scale attack to prevent us from cultivating this virtue. Here's why. A thankful person rejoices and trusts in God and receives everything as gift. Grateful people are thankful for everything they have and even rejoice in their trials, trusting that God will help them through their sufferings and bring good out of them. They are not easily tempted because they are happy with what they have. The prideful person, however, has a hard time being thankful to anyone other than himself. That's why the devil tempts us to be haughty, self-righteous, and ultimately unthankful. Think of Adam and Eve. They went from trust and gratitude to doubt and pride because of the lies of the devil.

A Corresponding Beatitude

Jesus said, "Blessed are the poor in spirit, for theirs is the kingdom of heaven" (Mt 5:3). We saw in chapter 12 that this beatitude corresponds with humility, and humility is the virtue we need to practice to counteract the pride that causes ingratitude. People who are poor in spirit know their own nothingness, know that they owe everything to God. And that's why they are thankful and love God so much, which is the key that unlocks the door to His kingdom. "To be grateful is a characteristic of humility, and that in itself opens the heart to grace", said Father Francis Hoffman, J.C.D., executive director of Relevant Radio. "Gratitude naturally takes us away from ourselves and opens us to others and to God, and that always brings joy with it."[5]

Meister Eckhart, the thirteenth-century German mystic, said, "If the only prayer you said your whole life was 'thank you,' that would suffice."[6] One heartfelt thank you to God in recognition for all that

He has given you and done for you can change your whole life. Gratitude, in fact, is the beginning of the end of the worship of ourselves and the beginning of the worship of God. We go from humility to gratitude to worship to God's kingdom—in that order.

Eucharist Means Thanksgiving

When the early Christians met, they would break bread together and commemorate the Last Supper. They would do exactly what Jesus had done and had asked them to do, as Saint Paul explained:

> For I received from the Lord what I also delivered to you, that the Lord Jesus on the night when he was betrayed took bread, and when he had given thanks, he broke it, and said, "This is my body which is for you. Do this in remembrance of me." In the same way also the chalice, after supper, saying, "This chalice is the new covenant in my blood. Do this, as often as you drink it, in remembrance of me." For as often as you eat this bread and drink the chalice, you proclaim the Lord's death until he comes. (1 Cor 11:23–26).

Within a generation of Christ's death, this meal, celebrated each Sunday, became the principal means of worship for Christians, who believed it was a real participation in and celebration of the saving sacrifice of Christ. They would gather to pray and sing, to hear God's word and a teaching, and to celebrate what they had come to call the *Eucharist*, which comes from the Greek word for "thanksgiving". They gave thanks to God for all the gifts He gives us, and especially His body, blood, soul, and divinity that He offered for us on the cross and makes present to us at each Mass so that we can become like Him. That is truly something to be very, very thankful for!

You can say that being thankful is written into the DNA of Christianity, so to speak. We are called to be thankful, to count our blessings, and to share them generously with others. Thus Saint Paul wrote, "Rejoice in the Lord always; again I will say, Rejoice. Let all men know your forbearance. The Lord is at hand. Have no anxiety about anything, but in everything by prayer and supplication with thanksgiving let your requests be made known to God. And the peace of God, which passes all understanding, will keep your hearts and your minds in Christ Jesus" (Phil 4:4–7). Many of us feel we need more peace in our lives. Having gratitude and trusting in God brings us His peace, "which surpasses all understanding".

Gratitude and the Temperaments

Choleric

People with a choleric temperament have lots of energy and seek to accomplish big things. They tend to have an awareness of their strengths and talents and can do things with great enthusiasm. However, they struggle with pride and may not show proper gratitude to God or to others. They may assume that their abilities have been acquired through their own effort and are indispensable, while considering the contributions of others as less significant. In order to see their strengths as gifts and to appreciate the gifts of others, cholerics need to counter-act their pride by training themselves in humility. They need to reflect frequently on all that they have been given. They need to accept their limits and failures and truly appreciate those who contribute their gifts and invest their time in helping them accomplish their goals. Cholerics are fundamentally challenged by humility and need to practice this virtue in order to thank God and others.

Sanguine

People with the sanguine temperament love people and are motivated by relationships. They also love adventure and are drawn toward things that delight the senses. They are naturally thankful for all they have, especially the people in their lives. However, they tend to seek out new things and experiences to the detriment of their content-ment with what they already have. Sanguines need to deepen their appreciation of the gifts that God has given them. They are funda-mentally challenged by perseverance and need to cultivate gratitude in order to stay the course with their most important commitments.

Phlegmatic

People with a phlegmatic temperament are motivated by peace. They have a keen sense of justice and are naturally drawn toward healing and restoring any brokenness they encounter. Phlegmat-ics tend to be dispassionate and logical, which means that their gratitude may come from a sense of obligation rather than heartfelt appreciation. They also may hesitate to accept gratitude and expressions of thanks from others. They will often downplay their own gifts and contributions. Phlegmatics are challenged by the virtue of greatheartedness and need to cultivate gratitude for the gifts they have and can share with others.

Melancholic

People with the melancholic temperament are motivated by ideas. They tend to be deep and have rich interior lives. They appreciate the giftedness of others and often see in them things they may not fully know about themselves. However, melancholics are prone to exaggerate problems and challenges, and they often fail to see trials as gifts and opportunities to grow. They may focus on what they lack rather than being thankful for what they have. Melancholics are fundamentally challenged by initiating actions and taking risks. In order to develop the virtue of gratitude, they need to reflect on their gifts and talents and how God is already using them. They also need to learn how to be thankful for their limits and challenges, failures and trials, by seeing how God brings good out of them.

Associated Virtues

The virtue of gratitude is assisted and practiced more readily when accompanied by these other virtues.

- *Appreciation* is thankfulness for your gifts and those of others.
- *Detachment* is willingness to part with material goods to serve God and others.
- *Good Stewardship* is the proper care and use of the gifts of God.

Associated Vices

A lack of gratitude can manifest itself in many ways, and we must be careful of these vices if we want to grow in thankfulness.

- Pride—thinking too highly of yourself. *Steals the ability and the joy of being grateful to God and others.*
- Greed—grasping material things beyond what you need. *Steals the joy of being thankful for and of sharing one's blessings.*
- Envy—resenting the possessions or the successes of others. *Steals the joy of sharing in someone else's blessings.*

Practical Ways to Grow

That's the textbook stuff, but let us talk for a moment about gratitude in action, and what it takes to develop this virtue at work, at home, and in life. To have gratitude, a person needs to do three things:

1. Thank God, the source of all good gifts, for your life, your talents, and your possessions.
2. Thank the people in your life for all the ways they share their gifts with you.
3. Take nothing for granted and see everything you have as a gift, even your trials.

Practice being thankful daily. It is a good idea to take on the monastic practice of thanking God in the morning, at each meal, and at night before bed. Take stock of your blessings and thank God for them.

Think about your life, each breath you take, willed and given to you by a loving God, who is not distant but who draws close and seeks to be in relationship with you. *Be thankful for the gift of life and cherish it. And be thankful for God's gift of eternal life.*

Think about who you are today compared to your past. In what ways have you grown and in what ways are you still growing? *Be thankful for who you are and who God is calling you to be, and seek to become the best version of yourself.*

Think about your family and friends, the people who have been a blessing in your life. Your parents, your grandparents, teachers and mentors, your friends old and new, your spouse and children. *Be thankful for all the people who have contributed to forming you into the man or woman you are today. Honor them by practicing the good things they taught you.*

Think about your talents. Think of all the ways you have used those talents to glorify God and serve others. *Be thankful for your talents, and the talents of others.* Think about the created world. What a gift all of creation is to us. A gift that we are called to "till and keep" (Gen 2:15) to provide for our needs. The green grass, the stars in the sky, the rain that washes the land—these and more point to and praise the Lord (see Dan 3:28–68). Think for a moment of what a blessing the natural world is, and how awe-inspiring it is. *Be thankful for this incredible world that God has given to us. Care for it and treat it with respect and appreciation.*

Think about your material possessions: your home, your car, and all the amenities that make life a little easier and more pleasant. *Be thankful for all that you have and seek to use it in ways that build you into a better person who serves God and others.*

By practicing gratitude daily, you will build up this important spiritual muscle and be more capable of seeing the world as a gift. You will see others and the goods in your life as God sees them. You will be freer to accept and to rejoice in the gifts God gives you. And you will be more prepared to use your gifts to serve others and glorify God. *Want to be happier? Be more thankful!*

To grow in the virtue of gratitude, pray this simple and short prayer attributed to Saint Richard of Chichester, bishop (1197–1253):

Thanks be to Thee, my Lord Jesus Christ,
For all the benefits which Thou hast given me,
For all the pains and insults which Thou has borne for me.
O most merciful Redeemer, Friend, and Brother,
May I know Thee more clearly,
Love Thee more dearly,
Follow Thee more nearly,
Day by day.
Amen.[7]

18

Wonder

"The heavens are telling the glory of God;
  and the firmament proclaims his handiwork.
Day to day pours forth speech,
  and night to night declares knowledge."

—Psalm 19:1–2

The virtue of wonder is the habit of responding with awe to the beauty and the complexity of the world. Children are by nature full of wonder. Thus for them, wonder is not a virtue. As we grow older, however, we tend to lose our childlike wonder and must make an effort to marvel at God's creation. That's why Jesus told us that we must become like children to enter the kingdom of God: "Truly, I say to you, whoever does not receive the kingdom of God like a child shall not enter it" (Mk 10:15).

Wonder is an openness of the heart that helps us to receive more of the fullness of reality. Children don't need to hear the advice "Stop and smell the roses", but we do. We need encouragement to slow down, to perceive the beauty that surrounds us, and to praise the One who created it. Through the psalmist the Lord says, "Be still, and know that I am God" (Ps 46:10). The adoration chapel is an ideal place to be still and to contemplate God's glory.

Wonder requires the humble admission that while you know much, you do not know everything. In fact, in comparison to all there is to know, you know practically nothing at all. Cosmologists say that roughly 80 percent of the mass in the universe is dark matter, material that cannot be directly observed.[1] The truth is that even the most knowledgeable people among us know very little. Which is why Socrates, one of the wisest men who ever lived, could say with a straight face, "I neither know nor think that I know."[2]

Socrates also famously said, "Wonder is the beginning of wisdom."[3] The Bible says something very similar: "The fear of the LORD is the beginning of wisdom" (Prov 9:10). Here, the word *fear* means "reverence" or "awe", which is closely related to the wonder that leads us toward understanding. Wonder is a natural human response to the material world. We are born inquisitive. We innately want to know more about ourselves and the world around us.

This curiosity is not limited to what we can see, hear, and touch; wonder also draws our hearts and minds toward nonmaterial realities like justice, love, and God Himself. The virtue of wonder keeps alive your desire to know more about everything and to encounter the Creator of it all. As Saint Basil the Great (329–379) told those gathered in his church, "I want creation to penetrate you with so much admiration that wherever you go, the least plant may bring you clear remembrance of the Creator. A single plant, a blade of grass, or one speck of dust is sufficient to occupy all your intelligence in beholding the way in which it has been made."[4]

Science and the Church

Many people might be surprised to see scientific and theological inquiry linked together. There is a common misconception that science and the Church are at odds with each other. But truth cannot be in conflict with itself. Unfortunately, clergy and scientists sometimes forget that they have different areas of competence for knowing different kinds of things.

One day a small child asked her teacher why the dew on the leaves formed in spheres. The teacher explained fluid dynamics and properties of surface tension in terms that the young girl could understand. After she finished, the young girl nodded and said, "You have told me how it does it, but why does it do it?" The teacher added more details about the texture of the leaf and the effects of gravity.

The little girl nodded appreciatively, and said again, "But why?" The exhausted teacher had run out of ways to explain the complex process by which water collects in a droplet and adheres to the underside of a leaf. Finally, the teacher knelt down beside the little girl, looked in awe at the dew- laden leaves, and said, "I don't know why. Why do you think it does that?" The little girl responded, "Because it's cool" and went to go play with her friends.

"Because it's cool" is not the most scientific of answers, but it reveals something important. We are made to study the natural world with great enthusiasm, to discover how it works and how best to be in relationship with it. However, the deeper questions of why and what is the meaning and the purpose of things cannot be answered by science. To answer those questions, we need the help of philosophy and religion. Knowing more about the natural world should increase our wonder about it and encourage these deeper questions, but knowledge doesn't always do that. Instead, it can puff us up, and then our pride can blind us to the truths that lead to God and His intentions for His creatures.

There is a common myth that says the Christian faith is *anti-science*. Nothing could be further from the truth. Nearly all the greatest scientists over the past two millennia were compelled by the Christian belief that the world is orderly and knowable because it was created by God. Mendel, Newton, Copernicus, and Galileo were men of faith. The conflict between Galileo and Church authorities does not provide an accurate picture of the longstanding relationship between Christianity and science.

A fuller picture can be seen by looking at the Vatican Observatory, which sponsors telescopes throughout the world so that scientists can study the solar system and the deepest mysteries of space and time. Vatican astronomers date back to at least 1582, when Pope Gregory XIII relied on them to reform the calendar, which is the calendar we still use today.

For another example of the Church's relationship with science, one can look at the scientific organizations supported by the Vatican. It may surprise some to learn that Stephen Hawking, the great physicist and a self-proclaimed atheist, was a member of the Pontifical Academy of Sciences. When he spoke at the group's annual meeting in 2016, he credited the Catholic priest and physicist Georges Lemaitre (1894–1966) as the true father of the big bang theory.[5]

The Book of Nature

Galileo wrote, "The glory and greatness of Almighty God are marvelously discerned in all his works and divinely read in the open book of heaven."[6] His words echo these from the Bible: "The heavens are telling the glory of God" (Ps 19:1). Seeing the book of nature as a form of God's revelation is found in Judaism and in Christianity from its beginning.

Saint Paul wrote, "Ever since the creation of the world [God's] invisible nature, namely, his eternal power and deity, has been clearly perceived in the things that have been made" (Rom 1:20). "From creation, learn to admire the Lord!" wrote Saint John Chrysostom (347–407). "Indeed the magnitude and beauty of creation display a God who is the maker of the universe. He has made the mode of creation to be our best teacher."[7] Saint Augustine (354–430) said, "Some people, to discover God, read books. But there is a great book: the very appearance of created things. Look above you! Look below you! Note it. Read it. God, who you want to discover, never wrote that book with ink. Instead, he set before your eyes the things that he has made. Can you ask for a louder voice than that?"[8] Saint Teresa of Avila (1515–1582) explained that looking at flowers, fields, and other beauties of nature helped her to pray. "In these things, I found a remembrance of the Creator. I mean that they awakened and recollected me and served as a book."[9]

Wonder is the key that opens the book of nature to the scientist, the philosopher, the theologian, and the mystic. Faith and reason are not mutually exclusive. Faith that refuses to study the natural world and learn from it is blind. Science that refuses to accept that the material world is pointing to something beyond itself is deaf. But when faith and science complement each other they lift up the human heart and mind. In the words of Pope St. John Paul II: "Faith and reason are like two wings on which the human spirit rises to the contemplation of truth; and God has placed in the human heart a desire to know the truth—in a word, to know himself—so that, by knowing and loving God, men and women may also come to the fullness of truth about themselves."[10]

A Corresponding Beatitude

Jesus said, "Blessed are the pure in heart, for they shall see God" (Mt 5:8). A pure heart is free from the corrupting influences that entice a person to sin. Children have pure hearts, and that is why they are filled with the wonder that makes them so receptive to the people who love them, the world, and God. We don't want to be sentimental about children; they are born with original sin, and at an early age they begin to manifest the willfulness that leads us all eventually to sin. But when they are little, they are not capable of knowingly and freely choosing to do wrong, and they are therefore innocent.

The virtue of wonder is exercised whenever we take pure delight in the natural world and the mysteries of God. Wonder involves joyfully beholding something just because it's there, like a sunset or a puppy, not grasping at something in order to possess it. When we wonder, we see the world not as a problem to be solved or something hidden waiting to be discovered and owned, but as an invitation to come and see. Wonder leads us to give thanks and praise to God for the goodness of His creation.

Wonder is an undervalued virtue. In this fast-paced, highly materialistic modern world, we need wonder more than ever. We must make time to encounter nature, others, and God in all the ways He is showing Himself to us. We must not take for granted the beauty, complexity, and goodness of the world, but rather try to hear what God is trying to tell us through it. Stay curious, cultivate wonder, and be awed by the creativity of our loving Father. In simple terms, we must remember to *stop and smell the roses* and to ponder God, who created them and us!

Wonder and the Temperaments

Choleric

People with a choleric temperament have lots of energy and seek to accomplish big things. They tend to have an awareness of their strengths and talents and can do things with great enthusiasm. However, they tend to move quickly and to focus on how to get things done. The classic line from Dr. Ian Malcolm in the novel *Jurassic Park* comes to mind: "Your scientists were so preoccupied with whether they could, that they didn't stop to think if they should."[11] Cholerics can be so focused on overcoming problems or achieving goals, that they never really learn to contemplate. They need to cultivate a sense of wonder in order to see the world and others not as problems to be solved but as marvelous creations of God.

Sanguine

People with the sanguine temperament love people and are motivated by relationships. They also love adventure and are drawn toward things that delight the senses. They can deeply appreciate the natural world but need to be careful not to treat it as merely a means to an end. They tend to feel they know things after just one meeting or encounter. They need to cultivate a greater sense of wonder and a willingness to go beyond surface knowledge.

Phlegmatic

People with a phlegmatic temperament are motivated by peace. They have a keen sense of justice and are naturally drawn toward healing and restoring any brokenness they encounter. They also tend to be more scientific and logical, and for this reason have a natural curiosity and desire to dig deeper into the questions we face. However, they can be dispassionate and so focused on finding a solution that they miss the opportunity for wonder. Phlegmatics need to build upon their initial sense of wonder in order to deepen it. They need to move from the questions of how and what toward the deeper questions regarding the meaning of things and their importance in life.

Melancholic

People with the melancholic temperament are motivated by ideas. They tend to be deep and have rich interior lives. They have the capacity to ask fundamental questions about the meaning of things. Their depth of thought and their ability to probe and examine mean that most melancholics have a deep sense of wonder. But, the virtue of wonder is more than an intellectual exercise. Wonder should move the heart toward appreciation and response. Melancholics need to develop the virtue of wonder by not only thinking deeply about things but also allowing their thoughts to move their hearts toward appreciation and action.

Associated Virtues

The virtue of wonder is assisted and practiced more readily when accompanied by these other virtues.

- ◦ *Inquisitiveness* is wanting to know the origin and the purpose of things.
- ◦ *Awe* is allowing your heart and mind to be captivated by beauty and majesty.
- ◦ *Humility* is living in the truth about the limits of your knowledge.

Associated Vices

A lack of wonder can manifest itself in many ways and we must be careful of these vices if we lack wonder.

- • Intellectual Pride—thinking too highly of what you think you know. *Steals the joy of experiencing the fullness of reality with an open heart and mind.*
- • Cynicism—not allowing yourself to be moved by goodness, truth, or beauty. *Steals the joy of being enchanted by the beauty and the goodness in the world.*

Practical Ways to Grow

That's the textbook stuff, but let us talk for a moment about real wonder in action, and what it takes to develop this virtue at work, at home, and in life. To have wonder, a person needs to do these four things:

1. Admit that you do not know everything, that is, have intellectual humility.

2. Believe that the material world reveals beauty, truth, and goodness.
3. Desire to know what the world is for and how God is revealing Himself and working in it.
4. Look for the extraordinary in the ordinary.

Practice being filled with wonder. Here are some simple steps.

Intellectual Wonder

Take time today to consider the questions you have always wondered about. For example, How many stars are in the sky? How many hairs are there on the average person's head? Why are barns painted red? What makes a rose smell so good? Some questions may be small, some may be deep, some may be practical, some may be silly. That's okay. Let your sense of curiosity guide you.

Think about what you already know about your question. Come up with a simple hypothesis of what you think the answer is. Spend just a few minutes thinking through how you would find the answer. Whom would you ask? What book would you consult? What questions would you type into a search engine? Spend a few minutes trying to find the answer. Take time to appreciate that you were able to ask the question. Appreciate for a moment that there is an answer to your question. And if you find your answer, praise God that He has created the world in such an orderly and comprehensible way. Thank God that He has created you with the ability to ask the question and seek out the answer.

Existential Wonder

Take time today to consider a big question about yourself. It can be anything from Who am I? to What job has been my favorite and why? It can be any question, but it must be about you. Ask yourself: Why did I ask that particular question? and What does it reveal about me? What do I think the answer is?

Now, really examine your temperament, your past experiences, your quirks, your talents, and so on. Bring all that to bear on answering your question. Really meditate on the question. Perhaps there are other questions that have to be answered first before you can answer the question you began with. Fine. Go where it leads you.

Now, reflect on what you have learned about yourself in this simple exercise. Take a moment to praise God for making you as you are. Ask God to help you be more patient with yourself and to help you make the time to listen to the movements of your heart.

Spiritual Wonder

If you were to meet Jesus today, what would you ask Him? For the sake of this exercise you only get one question, and it must be a big one. For example, Why did you create the universe? or Is there anyone beyond forgiveness? Come up with a question. Now ask yourself, How do you think God would answer? How would you answer the question if a child or a friend asked you the same question?

Take this question to prayer. Ask God to reveal the answer to you, to point you in the right direction, or to give you peace in the understanding you already have on the subject. Meditate on this question. If you have a trusted source, seek out the answer there. Discern whether this answer makes sense and is consistent with a good, loving, and all-knowing God. Grapple with the difficulty, the mystery, or as the case may be, the paradoxical simplicity of the answer. Remember, knowledge does not take away our sense of wonder. Arrogance and pride are the enemies of wonder, presuming to know everything about the world without ever actually seeing it in all its fullness. You see, wonder has a way of bringing out the best in us. It reminds us to look at the world with the eyes of a child, but with the knowledge and the responsibility of an adult.

In Fyodor Dostoevsky's famous novel *The Idiot*, the main character, Prince Myshkin, reflects on wonder. People think that because he is frail and sickly, he is feeble and numb to the problems of the world. They consider him an idiot, a simple-minded person. However, as the story progresses, we learn that he is the only one who is capable of seeing the world as it truly is. He says,

> Do you know I do not know how one can walk by a tree and not be happy at the sight of it? How can one talk to a man and not be happy in loving him! Oh, it is only that I'm not able to express it.... And what beautiful things there are at every step, that even the most hopeless man must feel to be beautiful! Look at a child! Look at God's sunrise! Look at the grass, how it grows! Look at the eyes that gaze at you and love you![12]

Prince Myshkin has the virtue of wonder, and it allows him to see the world as it is, and what it could be if we all lived in accord with our true nature. People who have the virtue of wonder are not naïve or idealistic, they are courageous and patient, and willing to look at things afresh and with the eyes of a child. Albert Einstein said that the person "who can no longer pause to wonder and stand rapt in awe, is as good as dead: his eyes are closed."[13]

By practicing the virtue of wonder each day, you will build up this important spiritual muscle and be more capable of being filled with awe and appreciation. You will see the world as a beautiful revelation of God, and you will better understand your place in it. You will be freer and more prepared to encounter the beauty and the goodness of this world with a pure heart and an open mind.

Slowly pray this prayer attributed to Father Pedro Aruppe, S.J., superior general of the Society of Jesus:

Fall in Love

Nothing is more practical than
finding God, than
falling in Love
in a quite absolute, final way.
What you are in love with,
what seizes your imagination, will affect everything.
It will decide
what will get you out of bed in the morning,
what you do with your evenings,
how you spend your weekends,
what you read, whom you know,
what breaks your heart,
and what amazes you with joy and gratitude.
Fall in Love, stay in love,
and it will decide everything.[14]

19

Cooperation

"Behold, how good and pleasant it is
when brothers dwell in unity!"

—Psalm 133:1

The virtue of cooperation is the habit of working with others toward a common goal that cannot be achieved by an individual alone. It is the virtue needed in order to get things done in community. Cultural anthropologists tell us that cooperation is at the root of all the greatest human achievements. Cooperation is deeply human. While other animals, from bees to baboons, work together for a common goal, they are motivated by their survival instincts. Human beings, however, cooperate not just to survive but to create, to advance, and to become more human.

It is amazing what we can accomplish together. God designed us this way. We are not islands, and we cannot live or create by ourselves. Our very existence is dependent on the cooperation and momentary unity of two people, our parents. We are born in the community created by our parents—their marriage, which is the foundation of the family—and we are made for community. While creating the human race, God said, "It is not good that the man should be alone" (Gen 2:18). And then He created male and female. In other words, we were made to be in relationship. We were made for communion with others not just for survival but in order to become who we are, as created in the image of God, who is a communion of Persons— Father, Son, and Spirit.

We could bore you with interesting studies that demonstrate we are social beings who need interpersonal relationships to flourish:

studies showing that we have the longest infancy and require more parent care than any other mammal, or that children tend to share without being taught, or that during crimes and accidents caught on video over 90 percent of the time strangers intervened to help.[1] We won't cite studies. Rather, we will just say it is a fact that *we need each other, not just to live, but to be human.*

Examples of Cooperation

When Neil Armstrong successfully piloted the Lunar Lander to a small rocky patch of moon in 1969, the entire fate of the Apollo 11 project rested on one man. However, his achievement was made possible not by his efforts alone. Nearly four hundred thousand people worked on the Apollo project at its height. Engineers, scientists, doctors, programmers, secretaries, caterers, and so on brought together their various gifts and talents in order to land a man on the moon.[2] The reason for investing so much money, time, and resources was not simply our survival. While the Russians had beaten us into outer space, and that posed a threat to our national security, the American space program was also an endeavor of curiosity, imagination, and ingenuity, which exalted the human spirit.

Big projects are not the only examples of cooperation. Little, simple activities can be profound examples of cooperation too. Two people paddling a canoe require as much cooperation and concentration as ninety people playing music in a full orchestra, even though playing symphonic music requires much more training and skill. We see examples of cooperation all around us, from family members doing chores around the house, to baseball players practicing for a game, to factory workers building cars.

It is important to distinguish between cooperation, which forms a community in order to reach a common goal, and a mutually beneficial exchange. The colloquial saying "I scratch your back and you scratch mine" illustrates an exchange that is more transactional, like making a trade for something, than communal. Cooperation, on the other hand, is more like "I have a ladder and you aren't scared of heights, let us pick some apples together." Before you dismiss that horrible analogy, we know a married couple who met this way. The point is, cooperation happens when people join together their unique gifts and talents in a common task. Not all mutually beneficial activities require cooperation in this sense, but all cooperation has a mutual benefit. However, while simple mutually beneficial transactions are easy, cooperation is hard.

The virtue of cooperation involves making a gift of ourselves and trusting others to make a gift of themselves. It is an exchange of persons, not just things. I bring myself, my talents, my skills, my wants, and my expectations. You bring yours, and together we work toward something better than we could achieve on our own. It is in this exchange that the bonds of community are built. Cooperation unites people together in powerful and dynamic ways. The more we cooperate with others, the more we also seek to be in unity with them, to have the same heart and mind as theirs.

Cooperation in Scripture

Jesus prayed at the Last Supper, "Holy Father, keep them in your name, which you have given me, that they may be one, even as we are one" (Jn 17:11). The New Testament describes how hard the first Christians worked at cooperation to achieve the unity God desired for the Church. Paul exhorted members of the early Church to "stand firm in one spirit, with one mind striving side by side for the gospel" (Phil 1:27). He prayed that God would grant them to live in "harmony with one another, in accord with Christ Jesus" (Rom 15:5).

The Church is the Body of Christ because through Baptism Christians are united with Christ and with one another. To stress the importance of cooperation, Saint Paul compared the Church to a physical body with different parts and organs working together. "For just as the body is one and has many members, and all the members of the body, though many, are one body, so it is with Christ. For by one Spirit we were all baptized into one body. . . . If the whole body were an eye, where would be the hearing? If the whole body were an ear, where would be the sense of smell? But as it is, God arranged the organs in the body, each one of them, as he chose. If all were a single organ, where would the body be? As it is, there are many parts, yet one body" (1 Cor 12:12–13; 17–20).

Paul used this analogy of a physical body to encourage Christians to use their various gifts for the good of all. "For as in one body we have many members, and all the members do not have the same function, so we, though many, are one body in Christ, and individually members one of another. Having gifts that differ according to the grace given to us, let us use them" (Rom 12:4–6). The gifts we bring are diverse, and together they achieve things we could never achieve as individuals. "Now there are varieties of gifts, but the same Spirit; and there are varieties of service, but the same Lord; and there are varieties of working, but it is the same God who inspires them all in every one. To each is given the manifestation of the Spirit for the common good" (1 Cor 12:4–7).

Cooperating with others is not easy, because everyone has not only different gifts but also different opinions about what things ought to be done and how. As we have been exploring throughout this book, people have different temperaments. Although God created all of us to work with others, we sometimes clash. And let's not forget the effects of original sin that damage our ability to set aside our egos and preferences for the sake of unity. That's why we need the wisdom and the example of the saints.

Cooperation and the Saints

Saint Benedict (480–547) could be the patron saint of cooperation. As a young man from a high-ranking family, he was educated in Rome, but he left the city to live a simple life in a smaller town. There his holiness became well known, and people sought his wisdom. He eventually moved to a cave in Subiaco, where he retreated from the world for a while. During his time as a hermit, he grew in self-knowledge and knowledge of the ways of God.

When the head of a nearby monastery died, the monks begged Benedict to be their abbot, and he reluctantly agreed. Despite his best efforts to lead the community in an orderly way, the monks rejected him and ultimately tried to poison him! Benedict left the community and founded twelve monasteries with a superior and twelve monks in each one.

To govern their way of life, he wrote his famous Rule. At the heart of the Rule is the motto *ora et labora* (to pray and to work). All of the members of a Benedictine community do these things together, using their talents in the service of the common good. The Rule became the foundation upon which many other Western European monastic communities were built. Benedict's twin sister, Scholastica, founded monasteries for women based on the same Rule.

Throughout Western Europe, monasteries became centers of learning and caring for the sick and the poor. Villages formed around them and their agricultural, educational, and economic endeavors. When the Roman Empire began crumbling, and the future of Western culture was uncertain, monasteries kept it alive. Even to this day, Benedictine and other monasteries throughout the world continue to be places where men live together cooperatively as brothers, or women as sisters, in service of one another and their surrounding communities.

There are lots of pithy quotes about cooperation, teamwork, unity, and so on that are used by sports teams, companies, and other organizations to lift morale. One of the more commonly used quotes is this one from Helen Keller: "Alone we can do so little, together we can do so much."[3] For Christians, cooperation should be a given, a basic part of loving others and being in communion with them. So Catholics and other Christians pass around on social media snappy quotes of their own, like this paraphrase of something said by Mother Teresa: "I can do things you cannot, you can do things I cannot; together we can do great things."[4] The point is, we are inspired by saintly people and heroic people whose lives illustrate the power of cooperation.

Cooperation and Solidarity

If you have ever picked up a stick lying on the ground, you know it can easily be snapped. But if you tie a number of sticks together, it is nearly impossible to snap that bundle. Cooperation provides a similar benefit. There is greater strength in multiple people working together, in a unified community, than in one person alone. This is the meaning of the word *solidarity*. Solidarity is based on the acknowledgment that we are all connected and dependent in some way on one another.

Solidarity was the name chosen for the Polish labor movement led by Lech Walesa, which helped workers to resist the tyranny of Soviet-backed Communism in the 1980s. While working as an electrician at the Lenin Shipyard (now Gdansk Shipyard), Walesa became a trade-union activist calling men and women to unite together to advance the common good. This led to his persecution by the Communist authorities, who arrested him several times. In August 1980 he was instrumental in helping negotiate the groundbreaking Gdansk Agreement between striking workers and the government. He then cofounded the Solidarity trade union to ensure that workers could continue their common efforts for their own good and the good of others.

When the Communist government of Poland declared martial law in 1981, it outlawed Solidarity and arrested Walesa along with many others. Several dozen Solidarity members were killed. This did not stop the trade union, which by then had become a freedom movement. It continued to grow, and with the support of Pope Saint John Paul II, President Ronald Reagan, and other Western leaders, the Polish people regained control of their country.

"We are all in this together." This is often what people say when they realize that they are in the same situation and try to band together to do something about it. We have seen this most recently during the COVID-19 pandemic with banners hung from balconies in Wuhan, China, Italians serenading one another from their doors and windows, and thousands of people in New York City banging pots and pans at the same hour to honor first responders and healthcare workers.

When people link arms for the sake of a common purpose, they often learn the necessity of setting aside some of their differences. A lesser-known saying of Martin Luther King Jr. summarizes this unity perfectly: "We may have all come on different ships, but we're in the same boat now."[5] At the root of such unity is not only solidarity but also empathy, and Christians are called to have both. "God has so composed the body ... that there may be no discord in the body, but that the members may have the same care for one another. If one member suffers, all suffer together; if one member is honored, all rejoice together" (1 Cor 12:24–26). God is calling the members of the Body of Christ to join together in unity to evangelize nonbelievers, battle our spiritual enemy, and help one another to reach the finish line of heaven.

A Corresponding Beatitude

Jesus said, "Blessed are the meek, for they shall inherit the earth" (Mt 5:5). Many people think of meekness as weakness. But meekness is strength under control. God Himself exercised meekness when He became a man and lived among us. His meekness is the example we need to have in mind as we try to cooperate with others. "Do nothing from selfishness or conceit," wrote Saint Paul, "but in humility count others as better than yourselves. Let each of you look not only to his own interests, but also to the interests of others. Have this mind among yourselves, which was in Christ Jesus, who, though he was in the form of God, did not count equality with God a thing to be grasped, but emptied himself, taking the form of a servant, being born in the likeness of men" (Phil 2: 3–7).

One enemy of cooperation is strong attachment to our own opinions and ways of doing things. Sometimes for the sake of unity we need to let go of our opinions and habits and to hold ourselves back from arguing or being uncooperative. The New Testament is full of examples of divisions among the first Christians. And in each case, the apostles called the Church to unity through a spirit of cooperation. Saint Paul warned Timothy, "Have nothing to do with stupid, senseless controversies; you know that they breed quarrels. And the Lord's servant must not be quarrelsome" (2 Tim 2:23–24). He wrote something similar to Titus and added, "As for a man who is factious, after admonishing him once or twice, have nothing more to do with him, knowing that such a person is perverted and sinful" (Tit 3:10).

There are lots of statements in Scripture that are difficult to accept at first. But hard sayings are often the most important for us to hear. Saint John said, "If any one says, 'I love God,' and hates his brother, he is a liar; for he who does not love his brother whom he has seen, cannot love God whom he has not seen" (1 Jn 4:20). The truth is, cooperating with others, in humility and with self-control, is the way we love them and serve the common good. If we can't cooperate with others, how can we expect to cooperate with God?

God seeks to be in a relationship with us. It requires true cooperation because we must freely bring our gifts and talents to participate with God's plan for us. The virtue of cooperation is indispensable for the Christian, as it is the best way to understand how we accept and participate in God's will for us and for those around us. We are not passive puppets in the hands of God, who is pulling all the strings. No, the all-powerful, all-loving God has given us free will and is constantly reaching out to us, guiding and asking us to cooperate with his grace. In fact, the degree to which we are happy, fulfilled, and holy, is in direct relationship to how well we cooperate with God's grace.

Cooperation and the Temperaments

Choleric

People with a choleric temperament have lots of energy and seek to accomplish big things. They tend to have an awareness of their strengths and talents and can do things with great enthusiasm. However, they are not always good at delegation and are prone to try to do things on their own. They struggle with sharing responsibilities with others in a spirit of cooperation and can fail to honor their gifts. They need to be sure that they do not place the task or the goal above the people who serve with them. The choleric needs to work hard at cooperating, especially in ways that highlight and strengthen the gifts and the talents of others. They also need to be sure to honor the contributions of others and give them credit for their accomplishments.

Sanguine

People with the sanguine temperament love people and are motivated by relationships. They also love adventure and are drawn toward things that delight the senses. They are natural people pleasers and can be great team players. In fact, they often prefer to work in groups rather than alone. They appreciate the giftedness and talents of others and will gladly delegate and share responsibility with them. However, sanguines are not always aware of their strengths and weaknesses and can take on too much. They can easily exhaust themselves and abandon the mission, especially if they aren't feeling appreciated or the group is not having fun. They need to discern carefully what gifts and talents they can contribute and commit themselves to the group and to accomplishing the task.

Phlegmatic

People with a phlegmatic temperament are motivated by peace. They have a keen sense of justice and are naturally drawn toward healing and restoring any brokenness they encounter. They are excellent team players. They know their talents and gifts and are happy to call out the gifts of others. They are also often realists about what can and cannot be accomplished. Phlegmatics do not often struggle with cooperation. However, they tend to avoid conflict and can be passively cooperative, that is, saying yes and just going with the flow. They need to cultivate active cooperation, asserting themselves and preemptively offering to help.

Melancholic

People with the melancholic temperament are motivated by ideas. They tend to be deep and have rich interior lives. They are not great team players primarily because they prefer to work alone. They can also exaggerate problems and challenges and tend toward pessimism. Despite this, they are loyal and long-suffering and can often outlast others in work and commitment. In order to develop the virtue of cooperation, they need to assess how they can help and then boldly participate. Like the sanguine, they need to commit themselves to the group as well as to accomplishing the project.

Associated Virtues

The virtue of cooperation is assisted and practiced more readily when accompanied by these other virtues.

- *Participation* is seeking to contribute what you can.
- *Teamwork* is valuing the opinions and the gifts of others.
- *Civility* is seeking to find common ground and being willing to discuss differences respectfully.
- *Solidarity* is sharing in a common mission with others.
- *Subsidiarity* is entrusting others with the work that rightly belongs to them.

Associated Vices

A lack of cooperation can manifest itself in many ways and we must be careful of these vices if we lack cooperation.

- Pride—thinking too highly of yourself. Thinking you are capable of a task without preparation or asking others for help. *Steals the joy of being honest about your weaknesses and relying on others.*
- Apathy—not caring about the well-being of others. *Steals the joy of working with others and forming friendships.*
- Cynicism—not allowing yourself to be moved by goodness, truth, or beauty. *Steals the joy of working together toward a common goal.*

Practical Ways to Grow

That's the textbook stuff, but let us talk for a moment about real cooperation in action, and what it takes to develop this virtue at work, at home, and in life. To have cooperation, a person needs to do four things:

1. Admit that you have gifts and talents that can serve others.
2. Serve others even without reward and sometimes at your own sacrifice.
3. Appreciate and willingly accept the gifts of others.
4. Commit yourself to being in relationship with others.

The virtue of cooperation is needed for joyfully working alongside others to accomplish things great and small. It requires believing that you have something to offer and willingly accepting the gifts and talents of others. Cooperation is what makes people team players who give their best and call out the best in others. It makes people capable of making simple acts of self-sacrifice to achieve a common mission. Cooperation is based on the belief that more heads are better than one and that forming community is as important as accomplishing the goal.

To grow in the virtue of cooperation, ask yourself the following questions:

1. In what practical ways can you be more cooperative with others in your life?
2. How can you be more cooperative with your spouse in attending to daily, weekly, and monthly duties?

3. How can you be more cooperative with your friends and colleagues in joyfully contributing and being thankful for the gifts and talents of others?
4. How can you be cooperative with the Lord, joyfully following His commands and being open and attentive to how the Holy Spirit is calling you to serve?

By practicing the virtue of cooperation each day, you will build up this important spiritual muscle and be more capable of working with others and forming community. You will develop your gifts, learn things about yourself, and accomplish tasks that you could not otherwise achieve on your own. You will be more open to God's grace in your life and more inclined to say yes joyfully to the promptings of the Holy Spirit.

Part 3

Your Action Plan with God

20

On Your Way to Holiness and Happiness

"I came that they may have life, and have it abundantly."

—John 10:10

The best guidance is given by people who have researched information in order to help themselves. We wrote *The WillPower Advantage* because we were seeking information about how to grow in virtue and looking for a road map to follow. Both of us also wanted to share our discoveries with our families and friends so that they could benefit from them too.

It all started one morning after Tom confessed his sins in the Sacrament of Reconciliation. When he heard the priest say, "Go and sin no more," he immediately thought, "How am I supposed to do that?" The priest didn't say, "Sin less frequently" or "Sin only if you can't help it." He said to *sin no more*. *The WillPower Advantage* was researched and designed as a tool to help us to sin no more. How? By replacing vices with virtues so that we can better align our wills with God's will for us.

When you practice aligning your will with God's will for your life, or said another way, if you invite God's life into your will, you will be filled with more joy, peace, and happiness. And who doesn't want that, right? But aligning your will with God's will is not easy. If it were, we would all be doing it really well already. Rather, it takes real work, true *discipline* (taken from the root word, *disciple*). It means knowing yourself—your strengths and your weaknesses, your temperament, your experiences, your dreams for this life and your hope in the next. It involves knowing who God is, how

He reveals Himself to you, how much He loves you, and what He is asking of you.

This book was written to provide some insight into the way grace builds on nature and the role we play in becoming the person God created us to be. It shares ways in which the saints, our ancestors in faith, overcame vices by growing in virtues. It is designed to give you a little more insight into who you are and how your temperament impacts your practice of various virtues. Above all, it is meant to give you some ammunition for the spiritual battles that wage within us and around us. The question remains whether you are willing to take the steps necessary to fight for a better you, the person God made you to be, and achieve the lasting happiness He offers you.

The Battle

Life on this earth is a spiritual war between good and evil, and the battles are fought in every mind and heart. God created you in His image to share His life with you, but at every turn the devil, the accuser and the father of lies, tries to separate you from God. To strengthen your resistance to his deception, below are several questions for you to answer. Think about them and respond to them. Let your yes be a resounding one; say it out loud if you want to. These questions are the first step in forming your will according to God's will for you.

1. Do you believe that you are created by God in His image to share in his life, and do you reject the lie that you are defined by your weaknesses and failures?
2. Do you say yes to those things that give life, joy, and peace, and no to those things that rob you of life, joy, and peace?
3. Will you work to develop the virtues you need to become the person God made you to be and to replace the vices that enslave and depress you?
4. Will you travel the narrow road that leads to happiness here and in heaven instead of following the crowd on the broad road of self-destruction?
5. Will you cooperate with God's grace to become the man or the woman you long to become?

The Winning Strategy

Now that you have declared your intention to fight this war, you need to commit to the winning strategy: building the virtues that provide lasting happiness, real peace, and authentic joy. How do you build these virtues, the *good habits* that you can use to replace your bad habits? First, by knowing who you are as God created you, which means understanding your specific temperament, gaining wisdom from your past experiences, and learning from your failures as well as your successes. Second, by practicing virtues daily. Here are the virtues we have described in this book:

- Compassion—sharing in the sufferings and the joys of others
- Prudence—making wise and healthy decisions
- Justice—giving others what they are due
- Self-control—behaving with moderation
- Courage—bravely responding to what each situation demands
- Humility—living in the truth about your strengths and weaknesses
- Obedience—doing what you know is right and what you ought to do
- Generosity—giving abundantly in the service of others
- Honor—recognizing your own dignity and acting accordingly
- Greatheartedness—trusting that you have been called to do great things and daring to do them with confidence
- Gratitude—giving thanks for all that you have
- Wonder—being filled with awe at the beauty and the complexity of the world
- Cooperation—working willingly toward a common goal with others

One way of thinking about these virtues is that they are the means by which you can become the person God intends you to be, the person who asks for and receives the life, peace, and happiness God wants to give His children. They are the means by which you can become the heroes and the saints your family, church, and community needs. We cannot develop these virtues by our efforts alone; we need God's help. And God is generous with His grace to all who ask for it. He readily answers the prayer: "God, please grant me what I need to become the person you want me to be and to fulfill the mission you have given me."

The remaining pages of this book will help you to design a customized strategy for your step-by-step growth in virtue. The suggestions we offer you are not based on science or pop-psychology. Rather, they are based on the wisdom that can be found in God's Word. If there is a science for living well, it is the "science of the saints", that is, the lessons the saints learned by walking with God. From the earliest days of the Church, Christians have relied upon the witness of the saints. "Therefore, since we are surrounded by so great a cloud of witnesses, let us also lay aside every weight, and sin which clings to us so closely, and let us run with perseverance the race that is set before us" (Heb 12:1). The saints, both those canonized by the Church and those known only by a few of us, attest to this truth: it is possible, with God's help, to become the person you were made to be, in God's master plan, in His image and likeness!

21

The First Step:
Three Questions and Four Truths

"Put off the old man that belongs to your former manner of
life ... and put on the new man, created after the likeness
of God."

—Ephesians 4:22–24

At the beginning of *The WillPower Advantage* you were asked three
important questions and offered four forgotten truths. The first step
on the road to more virtue, so that you can better conform your will
to God's will for you, is to reconsider these in light of the pages you
have read in this book and to make some decisions about them.

The Three Important Questions

Take a moment and answer these questions again. We encourage
you to write down your answers in the spaces provided below, on
a separate piece of paper, or on *The WillPower Advantage* website.
When we think and write at the same time, our ideas are more concrete and memorable.

1. How would the world be different if we followed Christ's
   teaching more completely?

   _____

   _____

   _____

2. What would change in my life if I followed Christ's words more faithfully?

_____

_____

_____

3. What am I going to do about it?

_____

_____

_____

Take your answer to question 3 and turn it into a clear statement of action:

I, _____, am part of God's incredible plan to put the broken world back together and reconcile it to Himself. I commit myself to the following actions:

With this commitment, I can better use my God-given gifts and talents to love and to serve God and others. I can do this only by cooperating with God's grace and becoming docile to the Holy Spirit. Jesus, I trust in You. So, please help me to know, to trust, to love, and to serve You more. Also, please help me to love my neighbors, as myself.

Signed: _____

Date: ___ / ___ / ___

There you have it! You are halfway through the first step on the road to more virtue.

The Four Forgotten Truths

The second half of your first step on the road is to review the Four Forgotten Truths from chapter 1:

1. God wants us to be happy.
2. The Christian life takes work.

3. Grace builds upon nature.
4. We were never meant to go through life alone.

Take a moment to reflect on these truths by answering the following questions:

1. What is one area of your life in which you would like to find more happiness?

   _____

2. What is an aspect of your life that you know needs more work?

   _____

3. What is an area of your life where you can see God's grace building upon and working with the person you are naturally, as in your gifts and temperament?

   _____

4. What is an area of your life where you turn to others for help (friends, family, colleagues, a support group, or a mental health professional)?

   _____

The area or areas you identified are where you need to practice the virtues more often. This is not a reason for discouragement, because these are the areas where God meets us with His grace and transforms us into the men and women He intends us to become. As Saint Paul said, God's "power is made perfect in weakness" (2 Cor 12:9).

22

The Second Step: Virtues and Vices

"For this very reason make every effort to supplement your faith with virtue."

—2 Peter 1:5

As we have seen, our unique temperament is an innate biological reality that is given by God and meant by Him to interact with our character. It is upon the foundation of our temperament and character working in harmony that our personality is built. Knowing your temperament is an important key to knowing yourself. Your natural disposition (temperament) along with your willed response (character) and the sum of all your experiences, make you the person you are today. Moreover, you can cooperate with God's grace in order to become the person He wants you to be tomorrow, and for eternity. Saint Augustine has been mentioned often in this book because he is proof that a person can change, even make an 180-degree turn, by being honest with himself and humbly surrendering himself to God. And let's remember to thank Augustine's mother, Saint Monica, who never stopped praying for his conversion.

The Spiritual Audit

The Spiritual Audit was designed to help you to grow in self-knowledge by determining your temperament and identifying both the virtues you have developed well and the virtues you need to practice more in order to overcome the vices that still challenge you. Go back to The Spiritual Audit in chapter 4 and answer these questions based on your list of strengths:

What are your top two strengths?

1. _____

2. _____

What are your bottom two strengths?

8. _____

7. _____

What are your top two areas of weakness?

1. _____

2. _____

What are your bottom two areas of weakness?

8. _____

7. _____

Now that you have read this book, do you wish to change any of these answers? If so, go back to The Spiritual Audit, answer those questions again, and copy your new answers above so that you have the most accurate snapshot of what makes you uniquely you, warts and all!

Understanding Your Vices

Your strengths are great gifts, and really, so are your weaknesses because they are opportunities to grow in virtue. It is important to remember that *not all weaknesses are vices.* Some of us are prone to weaknesses in some areas more than others. Some weaknesses are a result of our temperament or a lack of knowledge or experience. A vice, however, is a bad habit that we have acquired through repeated choices that take us away from being the best we can be. Vices steal our peace and rob us of joy.

Throughout this book, we reflect on the various vices and their effects in our lives. You must be honest about your vices if you want to overcome them by growing in virtue. So we suggest that you review the list of vices below, circle the ones that apply to you, and then number them in the order of how much they challenge you, with 1 being the vice that challenges you the most.

- Rashness—acting without thinking through the consequences
- Cowardice—failing to initiate action or to stay the course because of "what ifs"
- Laziness—failing to give the situation the attention and the effort it deserves
- Pride—thinking too highly of yourself
- Greed—grasping material possessions beyond what you need
- Envy—resenting the possessions or successes of others
- Lust—overindulging in sexual pleasure
- Gluttony—overindulging in the pleasures of food and drink
- Despair—lacking the hope that God will provide whatever you need to do His will
- False Humility—denying your abilities because of pretense, low self-esteem, or false notions of humility
- Anger—being overly displeased with a person or a situation
- Wrath—desiring vengeance
- Apathy—not caring about the well-being of other people
- Vanity—admiring yourself too much, especially your physical appearance
- Vainglory—excessively seeking attention, praise, and honor
- Intellectual Pride—thinking too highly of what you think you know
- Cynicism—not allowing yourself to be moved by goodness, truth, or beauty
- Small-mindedness—thinking too little of yourself and resigning yourself to mediocrity

What are your three most challenging vices?

1. _____

2. _____

3. _____

These are the vices robbing you of peace and joy. These are the habits that enslave you and hinder you from becoming the best possible version of yourself. By discovering and practicing the virtues that supplant these, you can become freer and happier.

Practicing the Virtues

The virtues conquer vices. Based on truth, virtues reveal the deceptions that vices feed upon. Vices are distortions of what is good, beautiful, and true. Like a circus mirror that distorts your image and makes you super fat, extremely short, or crazily thin and stretched out tall, vices present a warped vision of yourself. As good habits, virtues can replace the patterns of behavior that are robbing you of joy, peace, and probably your health too. The virtues directly counteract the vices by directing your energy, intellect, and will toward what is truly good for you.

In order to demonstrate the power of virtue to conquer vice, we turn to Saint John Damascene, who lived in the ninth century. He provides a clear explanation of this phenomenon. He discusses eight vices and how to eradicate them with their opposing virtues, while adding practical advice along the way. We have provided in brackets the names we have used in this book for these vices.

> These eight vices should be destroyed as follows: gluttony by self-control; unchastity [lust] by desire for God and longing for the blessings held in store; avarice [greed] by compassion for the poor; anger by goodwill and love for all men; worldly dejection [envy] by spiritual joy; listlessness [laziness] by patience, perseverance and offering thanks to God; self-esteem [vainglory] by doing good in secret and by praying constantly with a contrite heart; and pride by not judging or despising anyone in the manner of the boastful Pharisee (cf. Luke 18:11–12), and by considering oneself the least of all men. When the intellect has been freed in this way from the passions we have described and been raised up to God, it will henceforth live the life of blessedness, receiving the pledge of the Holy Spirit (cf. 2 Cor. 1:22). And when it departs this life, dispassionate and full of true knowledge, it will stand before the light of the Holy Trinity and with the divine angels will shine in glory through all eternity.[1]

Let us be clear, the vices are conquered and transformed into virtue when we are set free by the truth, purified by suffering, and strengthened by grace as we work on practicing good habits. Conquering a vice does not take anything away from you other than the false, distorted vision of yourself. You have nothing to lose but your slavery to the vice. Here is some really good news, a bonus of sorts: *one* virtue may conquer *several* vices, as can be seen in the following list:

- *Prudence* conquers rashness and cowardice
- *Justice* conquers greed, envy, and lust.
- *Self-Control* conquers lust, gluttony, anger, and wrath.
- *Courage* conquers rashness, cowardice, apathy, despair.
- *Humility* conquers pride, vanity, and vainglory.
- *Obedience* conquers laziness and pride.
- *Compassion* conquers greed, envy, pride, and anger.
- *Generosity* conquers laziness, envy, and greed.
- *Honor* conquers false humility and vanity.
- *Greatheartedness* conquers false humility, pride, cowardice, small-mindedness, and despair.
- *Gratitude* conquers envy and greed.
- *Wonder* conquers intellectual pride and cynicism.
- *Cooperation* conquers laziness, pride, and cynicism.

This list is not exhaustive, but it lines up the virtues we describe in this book with some of the vices they conquer.

Carefully look at the three vices you listed above. Pay attention to their opposing virtue. Which are the top three virtues you need in order to overcome your three most besetting vices?

1. _____

2. _____

3. _____

What would your life look like if you practiced these virtues more? Really think about it. Imagine the freedom! If you struggle with anger or gluttony or lust, imagine the peace you would have if you practiced more self-control. If you tend to be greedy, imagine the joy you would have by practicing compassion and generosity in sharing your blessings with others.

A man who struggled with anger once came out of the grocery store to find a younger man sitting on the hood of his car. His blood started to boil. "Who does this kid think he is?" he said to himself. He set his groceries down and started to yell at the young man, who patiently replied, "This is my car; your car is over there." He was right, and the older man apologized. Later the older man told this story to his men's group and asked them to pray that he would grow in patience and self-control. His good brothers in Christ not only prayed for him but challenged him to grow in those virtues by making the effort to practice them more often. This is exactly the kind of support we need from one another so that we will persevere on the road to becoming the men and the women God intends us to be.

The beloved Italian mystic Saint Pio (Padre Pio of Pietrelcina) once explained that practicing the virtues *takes time!* He highlighted the supreme importance of humility, being honest with ourselves, and charity, being patient with ourselves:

> Remain tranquil, striving ever more intensely with divine help to keep humility and charity firm within you, for they are the most important parts of the great building, and all the others depend on them. Keep yourself firmly fixed in them.... If we keep our hearts applied to the constant exercise of these [virtues], we will encounter no difficulties with the others. They are the mothers of the virtues; the other virtues follow them like chicks follow their mother."[2]

Do not be afraid to be honest with yourself and do not beat yourself up. Resist the temptation to discouragement by believing that God does not tire of giving you His grace. He wants you to grow and to become the person He meant you to be, and He will be faithful in giving you what you need.

Your Temperament and the Virtues You Need

In addition to being honest and patient with yourself, you also need to know two important things in order to practice the virtues you need in your daily life: 1) how your temperament affects your growth in virtue, and 2) how the virtues interact with your heart and mind.

234

How your temperament affects your growth in virtue

Below is a brief overview of the temperament combinations and the main virtues each one needs that we presented in chapter 4. Focus on your temperament combination, which you discovered by taking The Spiritual Audit. Caution, you are not defined just by your temperament. It is worth repeating that your natural disposition (temperament) along with your willed response (character) and the sum of all your past experiences, make you who you are today. Your temperament is merely the foundation on which your personality is built.

We name the temperament combinations for the purpose of illustration, not for the purpose of *labeling*. It would defeat the purpose of this book to say, "I am a pace-setter, and there is nothing I can do about it. That's just the way I am." No, you may in fact be a pace-setter, so know that about yourself, be aware of the strengths and the weaknesses you naturally have, and build upon that foundation to help develop into the person God created you to be. Temperament is innate, but it is up to you, with the help of God, to build the character you need to do His will. We must cooperate with God. He does His part, and we must do our part.

Choleric/Sanguine: The Pace-Setter

Common Vices
  ○ Pride, Rashness, Vanity, Lust, Envy
Virtues Needed
  ○ Humility, Self-Control, Prudence (as in Deliberation)

Choleric/Melancholic: The Problem-Solver

Common Vices
  ○ Pride (as well as Intellectual Pride), Anger, Cynicism
Virtues Needed
  ○ Humility, Cooperation, Compassion, Gratitude

Sanguine/Choleric: The Life-of-the-Party

Common Vices
  ○ Rashness, Pride, Lust, Gluttony, Vanity
Virtues Needed
  ○ Courage (as in Perseverance), Humility, Justice, Prudence